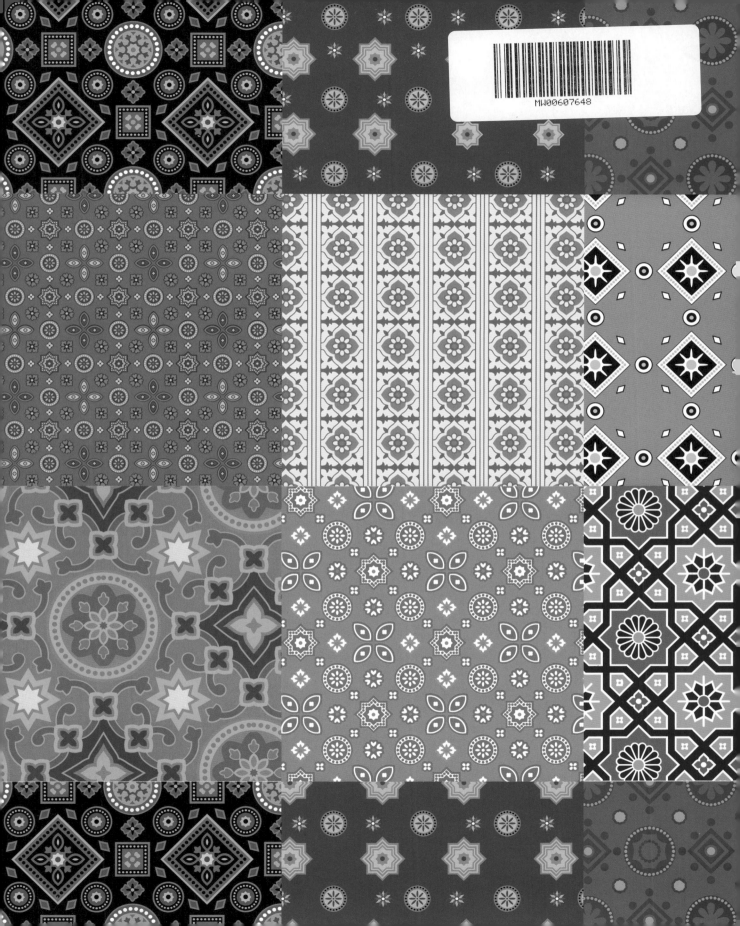

BEYOND MEASURE

Publisher Mike Sanders
Art & Design Director William Thomas
Editorial Director Ann Barton
Senior Editor Molly Ahuja
Designer Mumtaz Mustafa
Recipe Consultant Jordan Wagman
Photographer Igor Aldomar
Food Stylist Romain Avril
Assistant Food Stylist Lisa Zhong
Photography Studio Monogram Design Centre
Recipe Tester Bee Berrie
Copy Editor Monica Stone
Proofreader Claire Safran
Indexer Beverlee Day

First American Edition, 2024
Published in the United States by DK Publishing
1745 Broadway, 20th Floor, New York, NY 10019

The authorized representative in the EEA is Dorling Kindersley
Verlag GmbH. Arnulfstr. 124, 80636 Munich, Germany

Copyright © 2024 by Bilal Bhatti
DK, a Division of Penguin Random House LLC
23 24 25 26 27   10 9 8 7 6 5 4 3 2 1
001–337672–May/2024

A catalog record for this book
is available from the Library of Congress.
ISBN 978-0-7440-8841-0

DK books are available at special discounts when purchased
in bulk for sales promotions, premiums, fund-raising, or
educational use. For details, contact SpecialSales@dk.com

Printed and bound in China

www.dk.com

This book was made with Forest
Stewardship Council™ certified
paper — one small step in DK's
commitment to a sustainable future.
Learn more at
www.dk.com/uk/information/sustainability

Pakistani Cooking by Feel
with **GOLDENGULLY**

BILAL BHATTI

To Mama—thank you for being open to teaching me these recipes
that were passed down by Nani-Ami. I now understand all the hard work and struggle it takes
to make a meal for your family. I grew up eating your food and you taught me
there's more to a dish than just the ingredients—there's also love, care, and dedication.

And to Chef Jordan Wagman, thank you for playing an integral
part in helping me organize all my thoughts and explanations around
eyeball cooking into a digestible, readable format.

CONTENTS

INTRODUCTION

Welcome!

My name is Bilal Bhatti and I'm hoping to pass the wonderful Pakistani cuisine I grew up eating onto you.

I was born and raised in Toronto, Canada, where my parents immigrated to from Pakistan in the '80s. Throughout my childhood, the Food Network was my favorite channel; I especially loved *Iron Chef America; Emeril Lagasse; Diners, Drive-Ins, and Dives*...the list goes on. In my senior year of high school, I found myself trying to replicate Gordon Ramsay's recipes as well as those from other chefs I found on YouTube. I always enjoyed cooking, but I never posted anything online.

Fast forward to summer 2020. During the pandemic I found myself having more time at home just like everyone else. I also upgraded my home computer setup since I knew I was going to be doing a lot more remote work. With that in place, I was inspired to record and edit my recipes on my computer and share them on TikTok, just to pass the time and have a creative outlet.

I quickly found myself running out of ideas of what to cook given many of the dishes I made were just things I grew up watching and cooking from YouTube. These are also mainly Western-style dishes, so I thought to myself, I should really share the things that I eat daily i.e., Pakistani food! I knew what good Pakistan food was when I tasted it (thanks, Mama), but I didn't know how to make these wonderful dishes. It would be a shame if I wasn't able to learn to make the same dishes that my Nani-Ami (grandmother) taught my mother, so I decided to do just that and share it with everyone online.

I quickly learned that my mother does not cook with traditional measurements, as is the case with so many home cooks. Learning to cook by her side using my intuition has been vital to understanding how ingredients and flavors come together. It's been a challenge and a joy to implement the element of eyeball cooking into this cookbook.

Much love to you for wanting to learn this fun skill of eyeball cooking. I appreciate everyone who has supported me throughout my cooking journey and I hope to continue giving back as much value as possible.

How to Get Started with Eyeball Cooking

I create a ton of food content for social media. I am often asked by many of my followers about the exact measurements I use for my recipes, and the truth is, I don't use conventional measurements, it's all "eyeball cooking."

Put aside the tablespoons, cups, and the like (unless you're baking, as you generally need to be precise when it comes to baking) and start relying on your intuition in the kitchen. Eyeball cooking engages all your senses while helping you gain a better understanding of your ingredients. I encourage you to play with your food—that's the fun part about cooking, making every dish your own.

Practice makes perfect when it comes to eyeball cooking; it has taken my mother a lifetime to master, so be patient and enjoy the process. Instead of using traditional measuring spoons and cups, my mom uses fingers, palms, and standard household items. Whenever she'd ask me to add flour into a bowl, I'd use the same saucer plate, essentially creating a household 'standard' measuring tool. My mom would call for 'four saucers' of flour or 'one mug' of rice or 'pinches' of spices. And she's not alone—this is a common practice used intuitively by generations before her.

Although we don't use traditional measurements in this book, I encourage you to find useful items in your home and use them as a 'standard' unit of measure.

If you're trying spices or spice blends in a recipe for the first time, I would recommend having a taste. How do you like it? Is it too floral, spicy, or pungent?

Mix a little bit with another spice or two and taste again. This is where preference will come into play. For example, if a dish tends to lean toward the hotter end of the spectrum (in terms of spice level), the ratio of chili powder should be increased in comparison to the other spices. Try a little more of one spice this time and a little more of another the next. The flavor profile of a spice may also change depending on how it is cooked and how old the spices are that you're using. It's important to season and taste as you go to see if the flavor of what you are adding is coming through.

Eyeball cooking will take some time to get the hang of, but I promise, when you get there, you'll never go back.

Although many of these recipes have been passed down by my mother, I still find myself tweaking ingredients depending on how I'm feeling or what I'm craving. Some days I'll add more cloves and others a little more black pepper. I play with the recipes, and you should too! The more you do, the better you'll understand the ingredients.

Eyeball cooking is intended to bring the joy back to the kitchen. The process of creating a great dish takes time and dedication to reach a level of satisfaction. Forget about perfection—grab that spice, take a pinch, and throw it in a pot. Trust me, it'll be fine.

Here are examples of what I use in my kitchen:

For Flour: A saucer or tea plate. A full saucer equates to about 1½ cups, but again, we're eyeballing.

For Rice and legumes: An old mug that I don't drink from anymore. The one I use holds about 1½ cups of rice, but again, this will vary and that's okay.

For Spices: Finger pinches or an everyday tea spoon. Throughout the book I'll call for half a spoonful, a spoonful, or a large spoonful. This is not an exact science, but see the photo on the page below for reference.

For Meat: I tend to buy meat weighed by volume at the butcher and then "measure" in handfuls at home. If that's not something you're accustomed to, try to imagine a handful of meat is about ½ lb.

What Is "Pakistani Cuisine"?

To fully appreciate Pakistani cuisine, it is important to learn about the country's inception and the people who live there. Many people assume South Asian countries share many of the same recipes and are culturally similar, and although there may be some overlap, the cultures are vastly different.

Pakistan is extremely diverse—culinary influences differ from region to region, and the many cultures that dot those regions also have unique styles of cooking. Located in South Asia, Pakistan has four provinces and six major ethnicities. Pakistan is surrounded by Afghanistan and Iran in the west, China in the north, and India in the east—and you'll find culinary influences from neighboring countries in those areas. Pakistan became a country in 1947 after the British Colonial period, shortly followed by India's independence—where many Muslims in India migrated to Pakistan and many Hindus in Pakistan migrated to India.

Prior to British rule, many people within the Indian subcontinent identified with their ethnicity before most other things. For example, one would self-identify as Hindustani or Hindu (not the religion) and then maybe "Indian" under British rule. Only around 5% of India's entire population belongs to the same ethnicities that are native to Pakistan, mainly being Punjabi and Sindhi ethnicities.

With that being said, it can be difficult to label any one dish that can be found throughout all of Pakistan. Some Pakistani dishes can even be originated during the Mughal empire (1526–1857), with many formed and developed before and after the British Colonial period.

There are over 2,000 ethnic groups in South Asia and the differences are abundant within Pakistan. For example, my mother was born in Sahiwal within the Punjab province and grew up in Karachi within the Sindh province. She learned all her cooking skills from her mother who was also born and raised in Sahiwal. So my mother's style of cooking is traditional to those provinces. These are mainly the types of dishes you will find within this book, along with a sprinkling from some from other provinces or regions in Pakistan.

This is the food I grew up eating. Ever since I was a child, my mother introduced me to flatbreads—I got to taste the crispiness of a paratha mixed with the butteriness of ghee (see page 38). She opened my eyes to my favorite spiced rice dish, Lamb Pulao (see page 104), which I called "good chawal (rice)" when I was little. And she plied me with the sweet mango kulfi that got my sweet tooth going. For as long as I could remember, Pakistani cuisine has been a way for me to experience all my taste buds and connect with years of culinary traditions tracing back to the motherland.

Eating Basics

Congratulations, you cooked an amazing dish, it's seasoned to perfection and looks great! But, how do you serve and eat it? Properly serving and enjoying the meal the way it was intended to be eaten is crucial to experiencing your life's journey through recipes.

SERVING

For most of the dishes in this book, having a large dinner plate and a shallow bowl or pasta bowl should suffice.

Rice dishes are commonly eaten on large dinner plates, while dishes that have gravy or are saucier are easier to eat from a shallow bowl.

Growing up, the most common setup would include a large dinner plate on your right side for flatbread, and a shallow bowl in the center for your main dish.

Condiments are typically served in separate bowls and placed in the center of the table for everyone to enjoy. If eating alone or in more of a buffet-style setting, you may spoon condiments directly onto your plate, on the side, or on top of the dish; like Raita (page 129) over Lamb Pulao (page 104).

When it comes to most desserts, they're most commonly served in small bowls, given that Pakistani desserts tend to be extremely sweet.

USING YOUR HANDS

Whether it's for cultural or religious purposes, eating with hands is common throughout many parts of the world. At a young age, we're taught how to use spoons, forks, and knives... and if you're Desi, your hand too—the right hand to be specific. We use our right hand to eat because our left hands are meant for cleaning our private body parts. Many of the recipes in this book don't require any utensils, with the exception of dishes that are mainly liquid, like Kheer (page 150). Don't be a MADMAN and use utensils with Roti (page 28).

Flatbread
Let's use naan and kabob as an example. You generally want an even ratio of naan to kabob with every bite, so based on how big of a bite you want to take out of the kabob, match that size of naan and tear a piece off. Now while holding the piece of naan with

your index, middle, ring fingers, and thumb, you will cover a piece of kabob and tear it off while still holding onto the naan. So if you were to look at your hand, you have a piece of kabob snuggled inside of naan. Now you can simply dip a portion of this into some chutney and in your mouth it goes.

Rice

Eating rice with your hands can be a bit trickier as compared to eating with flatbread, but you'll get the hang of it in no time. With your right hand, use your index, middle, and ring fingers to separate a portion (think of how much you want to bite, like spoonful) of the rice onto the side of the plate. With the addition of your thumb, try to make this portion as compact as possible by mushing the pieces of rice together. Now with your three fingers and thumb, scoop up the portion of the rice. When placing it in your mouth, ensure your fingernails are pointed towards the ground so your thumb lays on top of the fingers. Use your thumb to push the rice into your mouth, like a little scooper. That's it.

It's also culturally accepted to clean off any remaining foods on your fingers with your mouth—finger-lickin' good. If you're eating a rice dish with some meat, follow these same steps but first break off a piece of meat you want to eat and add that to the portion of rice, and proceed accordingly.

Necessary Spices

Complex flavors, heat, and eating with your hands—you'll get used to hearing those concepts. Ideally, it'll be a good idea to buy the following spices in bulk as you'll constantly be using them. These spices will be commonly used in various dishes within this book. As outlined in the How to Get Started with Eyeball Cooking section (see page 12), if some of these spices are new to you, then have a little taste to get to know the flavor profile and experiment with the amount you choose to season with.

Growing up, we realized our parents would cook with whole spices, e.g., a stick/bark of cinnamon or whole cardamom pods and cloves—but they never removed them after the dish was done. Sadly, this left us with an unpleasant surprise of biting into a whole spice while trying to enjoy the flavours of a dish. If you want to be traditional, don't remove the spices when you're ready to serve, but I prefer to do so.

Chili powder: This is made from chilies that have been dried and then pulsed into a fine powder. Now, there are many different types of chilies that range in levels of spiciness. Typically we like our foods a bit on the spicier side, so aim for something that'll give a bit of a kick. The varieties used more often in Pakistani cooking are made from dundicut and Kashmiri red chilies.

Cumin seeds: A staple in so many dishes. They're earthy and a bit nutty. Cumin seeds can be toasted whole or ground into a powder and then toasted. My favorite way to use cumin is with lamb, as the flavors pair so well together.

Coriander seeds: If you leave cilantro to grow without harvesting, it'll flower and little green buds will appear. These buds will then dry up, leaving us with coriander seeds! They're a bit tart and citrusy.

Black peppercorns: Salt's best friend—I'm sure we all have this in our spice cabinet. I highly recommend you buy the peppercorns whole and toss them in a spice grinder. The flavor and aroma of freshly ground black pepper versus pre-ground is night and day.

Cinnamon: There are different types of cinnamon sticks/barks out there, the most popular ones available in North America being cassia and ceylon. My family typically prefers ceylon—specifically ceylon bark. This resembles the bark of a tree.

Green cardamom pods: This might be my favorite spice. It's a bit fruity and minty. We use these in so many recipes from rice dishes to meat. But my favorite way to implement this would be in chai.

Black cardamom pods: Not used quite as often whole as the green variety, but rather a key component in ground spice blends. It has a unique smoky menthol flavor.

Cloves: A little goes a long way! Cloves have a warm and bitter flavor. Sprinkle a few pieces in your basmati rice along with some cumin and you'll thank me later.

Black caraway seeds: These have a unique flavor combination of onion and oregano. Great in Paratha (see page 38) fillings!

Dried fenugreek leaves: The aroma surprisingly is similar to dark chocolate, and also has a bitter earthy flavor. Used in spice blends as well as garnish.

Ajwain (carom seeds): If thyme and oregano had a child, its name is ajwain. Its aroma is quite strong, so be careful not to overdo it.

Basil seeds: Honestly speaking, I don't smell or taste much of anything from basil seeds, but I do like how they thicken up and create a gooey barrier around themselves when soaked in water. They adds a great texture to desserts like Falooda (page 158)!

Fennel seeds: These have a refreshing floral and licorice flavor profile. Great in spice blends and chai. I also like candy-coated fennel seeds, which can be a great little snack.

Dried mint: This smells refreshing, just like a piece of mint gum. I love to incorporate this in different chutneys and the Pani Puri sauce (page 134).

Spice Blends

Garam Masala: This is one of the most popular spice blends we use. Garam means "hot" and masala means "spice." Think of this as a nice foundation level of spices so we can get a hint of loads of different flavors together. After this is added, feel free to add additional spices that you prefer more of. Every home has its own variation of garam masala with different ratios. The recipe you find here is the one used by my mother, so feel free to experiment and make it your own.

Lightly toast the following whole spices until fragrant (start with a few pinches of each and taste to find a ratio that works for you): cinnamon, cumin seeds, coriander seeds, black peppercorns, black cardamom pods (I typically use less), and cloves. Blend into a powder and store.

Ground Cumin and Coriander: A classic flavor combination, cumin and coriander go so well together. Sometimes you may not need a complex spice blend like garam masala, so if you want to tone it down a bit then this is the way to go.

Lightly toast a few equal pinches of whole cumin and whole coriander seeds until fragrant. Blend into a powder and store.

Chai Mix: This is my mother's chai mix! She needs to start selling this. It's a one-stop-shop for all your chai flavor needs. Instead of opening multiple jars or bags, just take a couple of spoonfuls out or carefully pick out what you want and add it into boiling water. The smell of all these spices when mixed together is amazing.

See page 192 for a full rundown on how to make this incredible blend.

Chaat Masala: A fun, spicy, and tangy blend. My favorite way to use this is on Chaat Masala Corn (page 132). The addition of mango powder and black salt really opens up your tastebuds on the sides of your tongue!

Lightly toast the following whole spices until fragrant (start with a few pinches of each and find a ratio that works for you): mango powder, black salt, dried mint leaves, chili powder, sea salt (I tend to add slightly less salt in comparison to everything else), coriander seeds, ajwain [carom seeds], cumin seeds, and Garam Masala (see above). Blend into a powder and store.

Necessary Ingredients

There will be a lot of recurring ingredients found in some of these recipes. Similar to how a mirepoix or sofrito can be a base for a lot of French or Italian dishes, we also have a combination of different ingredients and spices that creates a wonderful base for many dishes. If they are in your fridge or cupboard, there's a good chance you may not even need to go grocery shopping—or at the very least, only need to grab a few ingredients to complete the dish.

Ginger, Turmeric, and Garlic Paste (see page 60): The Pakistani Trinity (or at least that's what I call it). This is the foundation that most Pakistani main dishes are built upon.

White onions: Onions make everything so flavorful and juicy. It creates a nice foundation as it absorbs spices and stocks in many dishes.

Green Thai chili peppers: We like our food spicy and this is definitely the only chili we recommend! They may be tiny, but they pack a punch. Take a little nibble and proceed with caution.

Cilantro: Our go-to garnish. We don't really use parsley. For those who have that condition where cilantro taste like soap, I'm sorry. But this is all we use! It has a nice refreshing citrusy flavour and is used in everything from rice dishes to meat and veggie dishes.

Plain yogurt: We tend to use yogurt in many of our sauces, chutneys, and also as a method of marinating meat with other spices.

Milk and cream: Milk is used in many desserts and also in chai. (Don't forget about kulfi.) While we don't tend to use cream as much in dishes apart from maybe saag paneer or if you find a dish is a bit on the spicer end, feel free to cool it off with a splash of cream.

Ghee (clarified butter): Used as a beginning fat to cook our dishes. Another common fat can be a neutral oil like vegetable oil, but ghee just adds this nice buttery flavour that can't be competed with.

Lentils (yellow, red, white, brown): There are so many types of daal (lentils) out there. We'll be using different types and colors for different recipes—along with a blend cooked together in what's probably my favorite meal, Haleem (see page 80).

Split chickpeas: This is formed when the chickpea is split and husked. They add a great bite as compared to a typical lentil.

Basmati rice: The only rice we use! This is the king of rice in my opinion. It's long-grain, light, and fluffy. Unlike many short grained rice found in East Asia where they prefer it to be clumped together, Pakistanis need our basmati rice to be separate. If it's clumped together, you made a mistake and need to redo it!

Atta (wholemeal wheat flour): Not to be confused with "whole wheat" flour. Atta is a blend generally consisting of durum flour, wheat, bran, and wheat flour.

Besan/gram flour: This is a staple in pakora (fried fritters). To make a pakora batter, you need besan. Its flavour is a bit earthy and nutty.

Protein: Whether it's chicken, beef, or lamb, many of the classic recipes will have some sort of a meat component to them. These can be available at your local supermarket or butcher shop. To make things as traditional as possible, you may step into a Pakistani supermarket and ask the butcher for assistance. Generally, they know recipes and which cut you'll precisely need. For example, if you were to make Beef Nihari (page 74), all you need to say is, "2 pounds of beef nihari meat," and they'll know exactly what part of the cow to trim from.

Necessary Equipment

Make your life easy in the kitchen and grab the right tools. Having the correct equipment will also make cooking more fun as you won't be worried about potentially messing up part of the recipe because you don't have the right tool for the job. These pieces of equipment will help bring out the best in a dish.

Tawa: This is a large, flat pan that's generally used to cook flatbreads, such as Roti (page 28) and Paratha (page 38). Unlike other pans, there isn't a rim on a tawa, which makes it easy to slap on a flatbread without it being caught by an edge. This type of pan also makes it easy to rotate flatbreads while they're cooking. They're typically made from cast iron or aluminum and come in 8-inch (20 cm) and 12-inch (30.5 cm) diameters, which means they're made for cooking a single flatbread at a time. If you don't have access to a tawa or would prefer not to buy one, a crepe pan or any other flat, rimless pan will do the trick.

Karahi: Think of a karahi as wok but with a large base. Traditionally in Pakistan, karahis don't have any handles and are handled by experienced chefs who use large metal tongs to rotate them on the stove. But at home, we can just use a medium-large sized deep dish pot.

Pressure cooker: Although it's not necessary, I highly recommend getting yourself one of these to cut down on the cooking time of many dishes you'll find in the Classics chapter (see page 58). I prefer to use the stovetop variety for optimal searing. Regardless, whether you're using an electric or stovetop version, it's important to ensure the lid is fully secured so no air escapes through the sides.

Blender and hand blender: Any blender should do. We'll typically use these for drinks, kulfis, and other dishes to ensure the consistency becomes smooth.

Food processor: A really versatile piece of equipment in the kitchen and we'll be using this in many recipes—from flatbread fillings to kabobs and chutneys. A food processor will make your life much easier. You could also go the manual route and use a mortar and pestle which can create a nice rustic texture—it'll also give you a nice arm workout, but it'll just take longer.

Rolling pin: There are many different styles and shapes. My mother always uses one that has handles attached to the main rolling pin, but any type will do. It took me years to master using the rolling pin. Mama always told me to be light with my hands and let the rolling pin do the work. Practice makes perfect!

Kulfi mold: I recommend using the silicone ones as opposed to the plastic molds because they are much easier to remove. All you have to do is fold away the mold and pull out the pops. If you are using the plastic molds, you may need to twist or dip it in warm water to try and pull out the kulfis.

Rubber spatula: This is a great tool to have in your kitchen. This is especially important for making your kulfi base because you want to make sure no milk gets stuck to the bottom and sides of your pan and gets burned. With a rubber spatula you're able to scrape all sides of the pan and ensure nothing gets left behind.

Tongs: You'll need these for many dishes, especially the Flatbreads (see page 26)—unless you're like Mama who bravely uses her hands!

Spider/slotted spoon: Not only are these great for frying by ensuring excess oil drips away, they're also helpful for mixing and scooping out rice.

Strainer: This is especially helpful for chai so we can remove remaining tea and spices from your drinking mug.

EYEBALL COOKING TOOLS

Saucer: Mama typically uses this to scoop atta into a mixing bowl.

An old mug: This can be used for measuring out rice or legumes.

Everyday tea spoon: We have metal ones and even leave plastic spoons in our spice jars to help us season whenever we need more than a pinch of something.

As mentioned in the Eyeball Cooking section (page 12), these are just items we use in our kitchen. Feel free to use whatever you have laying around in your kitchen and keep that as the standard unit of measurement for yourself.

FLATBREADS

There's a good chance that whatever dish you make from the book, it'll be accompanied by either a flatbread or basmati rice. We need some sort of carb to go along with these dishes, without it the dish would seem incomplete. If you serve any of these dishes to a desi, without anything to eat it with, they'll just stare at you and at the plate, sitting there... expecting you to bring out the roti or chawal (rice). Flatbreads come in all shapes and sizes, the common theme is that you break a piece off and use that to scoop up a part of the dish and then eat it.

Roti

It would feel strange to eat a classic Pakistani dish without roti or rice. Learning how to make roti feels like a Pakistani rite of passage. Roti is a family favorite and is the most popular flatbread made in our home. We enjoy using roti to scoop food and any remaining sauce on the plate. Knowing how much we love roti, my mother always had prepared dough in the fridge to be used at a moment's notice.

Yield: 8–12 large rotis
Prep time: 45 minutes
Cook time: 2 minutes (4 minutes per roti)

EQUIPMENT
tawa or any large flat pan

rolling pin

INGREDIENTS
5 saucers of atta (page 23), divided

pinch of salt

neutral oil, for cooking

TIPS

* Mama always cleaned the sides of her bowl while she mixed the dough. Be sure to scrape off any flour that gets stuck during this process and incorporate it back into the dough.

* Don't leave the roti circle on the counter for too long before cooking since it will dry out. Once it's rolled, get it into the pan ASAP.

* If you have a gas stove, you can try flipping the roti right onto the flame. This allows the roti to inflate and results in a fluffier roti. Be sure to constantly flip and move it around to prevent burning it.

1. Add 4 saucers of atta and salt into a large mixing bowl.

2. Make a well in the flour. Fill up a small jug or pitcher with water (keep in mind we may not need all of it) and add a small amount of water into the well. Mix the flour and water with your fingertips until a dough comes together, periodically adding splashes of water as needed to form a sticky ball. Cover the bowl with a clean kitchen towel and transfer it to the fridge for 15 minutes.

3. Remove the bowl from the fridge, and using your hands, begin kneading the dough by pressing your knuckles into it and aggressively hitting every spot. If the dough feels dry, you can add splashes of water to hydrate it. After roughly 10 minutes, the final product should be a soft, smooth dough ball that is dry to the touch (see Tips).

4. Transfer dough ball to a lightly greased container or bowl, cover, and rest in the fridge for 20 minutes.

5. Remove the bowl from the fridge, scoop out a palmful of dough, and lightly press both sides of the dough into the remaining saucer of flour.

6. Hold the piece of dough in one palm and using your fingers of your other, pull the perimeter into the center. Repeat this motion all the way around.

7. While still holding the dough in your palm, flip the dough to the opposite side. Cup the top of the dough with your other hand, and make a ball.

8. Place the dough into the saucer of flour, press to form a disc, and place the dough on your countertop or cutting board. Using a rolling pin, roll the dough into a circle, similar to rolling pizza dough. The end product should be thin but not transparent.

9. Preheat your pan over medium-high heat until you see a bit of smoke. Carefully transfer the roti onto the dry pan and sear for 30 seconds. Flip the roti, repeating every 30 seconds, rotating the roti with tongs to ensure even cooking. Continue cooking until the entire roti is golden brown and dark spots appear, about 4 minutes.

10. Remove the roti from the pan, transfer to a plate, and cover with a clean kitchen towel to keep the roti warm and moist. Repeat until all the rotis are cooked. Serve immediately.

STEP 2

STEP 2

STEP 3

STEP 7

Missi Roti

This chickpea-flour roti is denser than the typical wholemeal flour roti. Missi roti is perfect when eaten with a simple, sweet yogurt sauce. In my home growing up, we would mainly make traditional roti, so whenever a different style of roti was served, it was always a treat.

Yield: 4–6 rotis
Prep time: 2 hours 15 minutes
Cook time: 20 minutes (4 minutes per roti)

EQUIPMENT

tawa or any flat pan

rolling pin

INGREDIENTS

2 saucers of chickpea (gram) flour

2 saucers of atta (page 23), divided

pinch of salt

3 grinds of freshly cracked black pepper

pinch of cumin seeds

½ spoonful chili powder

½ spoonful black caraway seeds

olive oil

1 spoonful Ginger, Turmeric, and Garlic Paste (page 60)

1 small shallot, finely chopped

1 green Thai chili pepper (see Tips)

pinch of chopped fresh mint

pinch of chopped fresh cilantro

neutral oil or ghee

TIP

Don't be shy with the ghee when cooking roti. Ghee helps achieve a golden finish on the roti.

1. In a large mixing bowl, add the chickpea flour, 1 saucer of atta, salt, black pepper, cumin seeds, chili powder, caraway seeds, and olive oil and mix to combine. Fill a small jug or pitcher with water and periodically add splashes of it to the bowl until a smooth dough ball is formed.

2. Add the Ginger, Tumeric, and Garlic Paste, shallot, Thai pepper, mint, and cilantro. Mix until everything is incorporated and the dough is smooth.

3. Leaving the dough in the bowl, cover the bowl with a clean kitchen towel and transfer it to the fridge to rest for 2 hours.

4. Remove the bowl from the fridge and scoop out a palmful of dough. Using the remaining saucer of atta, lightly coat the palmful of dough.

5. Hold the piece of dough in one palm. Use the fingers of your other hand to pull the perimeter into the center and repeat all the way around.

6. Flip the dough in your palm and cup the top of the dough with your other hand, then twist to form a dough ball.

7. Using the remaining saucer of atta, press both sides of the dough into the flour and flatten to form a disc. Remove the flattened dough, and in

your palm, use your fingers to gently press the perimeter of the dough and flatten it even more.

8. Place the flattened dough on your work surface and use a rolling pin to roll the dough into a circle, similar to rolling pizza dough. The end product should be thin but not transparent and you should be able to easily hold it with your hands without it tearing apart.

9. Preheat a pan over medium-high heat until you begin to see a bit of smoke and then carefully transfer the roti circle onto the pan. Add oil or ghee over the top and cook until the top turns light brown. Flip the roti and cover the top with additional oil or ghee.

10. Periodically rotate and fold the roti with tongs to ensure even cooking. You are looking for brown spots to form.

11. Once the bottom is golden brown, flip and continue cooking until golden brown all over.

12. Enjoy the roti immediately with Yogurt Sauce (see page 42) or transfer to a towel-lined plate and cover with a cloth to them keep warm while cooking the remaining dough.

Makki Roti

I love rotis made with flours other than wheat, and this is one of my favorites. Made with cornmeal primarily, this roti is quite dense and incredible when paired with Saag (see page 87), a dish of slow-cooked greens.

Yield: 4 rotis
Prep time: 45 minutes
Cook time: 16 minutes (4 minutes per roti)

EQUIPMENT

tawa or any flat pan

rolling pin

plastic wrap

INGREDIENTS

3 saucers of cornmeal, divided

1 saucer of atta (page 23)

pinch of salt

large glass of milk

8 tablespoons room-temperature unsalted butter

TIP

Compared to regular roti, you'll need to be more careful when transferring makki roti to the pan. Cornmeal is less elastic than whole-wheat flour so makki roti can be prone to cracking or falling apart if not handled gently.

1. In a large mixing bowl, combine 2 saucers of cornmeal and the atta and salt. Fill a small jug or pitcher with water, then add equal splashes of water and milk to the flour and mix until a smooth dough ball is formed. The consistency of the dough should be similar to playdough.

2. Leaving the dough in the bowl, cover the bowl with a clean kitchen towel and transfer it to the fridge to rest for 30 minutes.

3. After resting, remove the bowl from the fridge. Sprinkle your work surface with cornmeal. Scoop out a palmful of dough and lightly coat all sides by rolling it in the remaining saucer of cornmeal.

4. Hold the piece of dough in one palm and using the fingers of your other hand, push the perimeter into the center of the dough. Repeat this motion all the way around.

5. While still holding the dough in your palm, flip it and cup the top with your other hand, making circular motions to create a ball.

6. On your work surface, lightly oil two large pieces of plastic wrap. Sandwich the dough ball between the plastic wrap layers with the oiled sides touching the dough. Using a rolling pin, roll the dough into a circle. The end product should be thin but not transparent and you should be able to easily hold it with your hands without it tearing apart.

7. Preheat your pan over medium-high heat until you begin to see a bit of smoke.

8. Carefully place the roti circle into the pan and generously add room-temperature butter to cover the top. (See Tip.) Cook until the top begins to turn a dark tan color. Flip the roti, cover the top with additional butter, and periodically rotate the roti with tongs to ensure even cooking.

9. Once all sides are browned, remove roti from the pan, about 4 minutes.

10. Enjoy the roti immediately with Saag (see page 87) or transfer to a towel-lined plate and cover to keep warm while cooking the remaining rotis.

Papar (Papadum)

This is the quickest flatbread I make, and it's basically a huge cracker. The trickiest part is rolling out the dough into paper-thin rounds. Growing up, my mother would typically buy the flattened dough from our local Pakistani market, so she would only need to fry the dough for a few seconds—and just like that, papadum! It's always fun to try and make papars at home too, so give this recipe a shot. The crunch can be quite addictive, so you'll definitely need to make more than one batch.

Yield: 4–6 papars
Prep time: 30 minutes
Cook time: about 2 minutes (10 to 30 seconds per papar)

EQUIPMENT

a large, deep, wide pot,
  like a karahi or a wok

rolling pin

INGREDIENTS

vegetable oil, for deep frying

1 saucer of chickpea (gram) flour

1 saucer of all-purpose flour

½ spoonful baking soda

pinch of salt

pinch of chili powder

pinch of cumin

2 grinds of cracked pepper

TIP

Roll out the dough near the stove to make it easier to transfer from countertop to frying pan.

1. Fill ⅓ of a large shallow pan with vegetable oil and set it over medium-high heat.

2. In a mixing bowl, combine both flours, the baking soda, salt, chili powder, cumin, and pepper, and mix. Fill a small jug or pitcher with water. Continue mixing the dough with your hands, while periodically adding splashes of water, until a dough ball forms. The final product should be smooth and quite dense. Cover the bowl with a clean kitchen towel and set aside to rest for 15 minutes at room temperature.

3. Place the dough on your work area and knead it with your palms and knuckles for a couple of minutes.

4. Grease your hands with oil and roll the dough into a log. Cut the log into four equal pieces and then roll each piece until it is the size and shape of a golf ball.

5. Use the rolling pin to roll the dough balls into large, thin flatbreads (they should look almost transparent).

6. Carefully lay the dough into the oil, away from you, to prevent splashing yourself with oil. Frying will only take 10–30 seconds. Flip the papar once halfway through the time.

7. Remove the papar from the oil and place it on a paper towel to remove excess oil. Enjoy immediately.

STEP 5

STEP 5

STEP 6

STEP 7

Paratha

I like to think of paratha as a superior version of roti: crispier, flakier, and laminated with butter. When you tear into it, you should see the individual layers just flake off. Every bite should include a wonderful crisp. Similar to roti, it's used as a vehicle to scoop whatever you're eating. Growing up, we would rarely have a meal without parathas or rotis.

I have such fond memories of my mother's parathas, she would always take the extra time to make them for me because she knew how much I loved them. I ate them every chance I could. Thank you, Mom.

Yield: 20 parathas
Prep time: 50 minutes
Cook time: 6 minutes

EQUIPMENT
tawa or any large flat pan

rolling pin

INGREDIENTS
5 saucers of atta (page 23), divided

pinch of salt

vegetable oil or ghee

heaping spoonfuls of room-temperature unsalted butter

1. Add 4 saucers of flour and the salt into a large mixing bowl.

2. Make a well (a small hole) in the flour. Fill a small jug or pitcher with water (keep in mind we may not need all of it) and splash water into the well. Mix the flour and water with your fingertips until a dough comes together, periodically adding splashes of water as needed until a sticky ball is formed. Cover the bowl with a clean kitchen towel and transfer it to the fridge for 15 minutes.

3. Remove the bowl from the fridge, and using your hands, begin kneading the dough by pressing your knuckles into it and aggressively hitting every spot. If the dough feels dry, you can add small splashes of water from the jug to hydrate it. After roughly 10 minutes, the final product should be a soft, smooth dough ball that is dry to the touch (see Tips, page 41).

4. Transfer dough ball to a lightly greased container or bowl, cover, and rest in the fridge for 20 minutes.

5. Remove the bowl from the fridge, scoop out a palmful of dough, and using the remaining saucer of flour, lightly press both sides of the dough into the flour.

6. Hold the piece of dough in one palm and using your fingers of your other, pull the perimeter into the center. Repeat this motion all the way around.

7. While still holding the dough in your palm, flip the dough to the opposite side. Cup the top of the dough with your other hand, and make a ball.

8. Press both sides of the dough into the saucer of flour to flatten into a disc. While holding the dough up, with your palm and fingers, gently squeeze the perimeter of the dough to flatten even more.

9. Holding the top and bottom of the disc, gently pull lengthwise to elongate the dough while lightly slapping it against the countertop to form an oval shape. This slapping motion will help elongate the dough gently and avoid ripping it.

10. Using your fingertips, add small dollops of butter across the top side of the dough and spread evenly. (See Tips, page 41.)

11. Starting at the long edge of the dough, use your fingertips to begin rolling the dough from the top of the dough toward the bottom to form a log. Carefully roll the log with your palms to make it longer, until it's about twice the length. Dip the log into the extra saucer of atta so it doesn't stick to itself.

12. Coil the log into itself like a snake, while periodically pressing the center so it stays in place. This is how paratha gets its flaky texture.

13. Place the disc on your countertop or cutting board and use a rolling pin to roll the dough into a circle. The end product should be thin but not transparent. You should be able to easily hold it with your hands without it tearing apart.

14. Preheat the pan over medium-high heat until you see a bit of smoke. Carefully transfer a paratha to the pan. Generously add oil or ghee to cover the paratha, and once the bottom has become dark brown, flip it. Adding more oil or ghee over the top, continue to cook the paratha.

15. Periodically rotate and fold the paratha with tongs to ensure even cooking and that brown spots are forming. Folding and making creases will also allow for some layers to open up and get even crispier.

16. Remove the paratha from the pan and enjoy immediately or transfer to a towel-lined plate and cover to keep warm while rolling and cooking the remaining dough (see Tips, page 41).

STEP 10

STEP 11

STEP 11

STEP 11

TIPS

✳ Mama always cleaned the sides of her bowl while she mixed the dough. Be sure to scrape the sides of the bowl to remove any flour that gets stuck during this process.

✳ One way to test if the dough is ready is to push down on it with your fingers. The dough should show a print and not immediately spring back.

✳ It's important to cook the paratha after you roll it out. Leaving the paratha circle on the counter for too long will cause it to dry out. Once it's rolled, get it into the pan ASAP.

✳ After adding the butter, feel free to sprinkle your favorite seeds (e.g., sesame seeds or even thinly sliced green onions). Experiment and fill your paratha to make it your own.

Aloo Paratha

This is a classic breakfast item, but I find myself eating this for dinner too. There's nothing better than a crispy flatbread stuffed with a spicy potato filling. Pair this with Chai (see page 192), and you're ready to start the day. The difference with this paratha, as compared to other parathas that aren't stuffed, or even roti, is that you don't commonly use this to scoop up another dish because it already has a wonderful filling. Honestly, you could eat this by itself, or what we commonly do is dip it in a sweet yogurt sauce.

Yield: 10 parathas
Prep time: 1 hour
Cook time: 6 minutes

EQUIPMENT

tawa or any flat pan

rolling pin

DOUGH

3 saucers of atta (page 23)

pinch of salt

glug of vegetable oil or ghee, for cooking

ALOO (POTATO) FILLING

4 small potatoes, peeled and boiled

1 palmful of chopped fresh cilantro

1 spoonful dried fenugreek leaves

2 spoonfuls dried mint leaves

1 spoonful chili powder

1 spoonful coriander seeds

1 spoonful black caraway seeds (nigella seeds)

1 spoonful cumin seeds

1 spoonful crushed red pepper flakes

1 spoonful salt

drizzle of olive oil

DOUGH

1. Add the atta and salt into a large mixing bowl. Fill a small jug or pitcher with water. Periodically add water and mix the flour with your fingertips until the dough comes together to form a firm ball. Cover the bowl with a clean kitchen towel and transfer to the fridge for 15 minutes.

2. Remove dough from the fridge and using the knuckles of both hands, knead the dough, periodically adding splashes of water when you feel the dough is too dry. The end product should be soft and smooth and dry to the touch.

3. Transfer the dough to a lightly greased container or bowl and rest, covered, in the fridge for 20 minutes.

ALOO (POTATO) FILLING

4. Add the boiled potatoes into a large mixing bowl and mash (with a masher or fork) until chunky.

5. Add all remaining filling ingredients and mix well to combine. Remember to taste the potato mixture and make any necessary adjustments to the seasonings. Set aside.

YOGURT SAUCE

4 heaping spoonfuls plain yogurt
splash of milk
pinch of granulated sugar
chopped cilantro, for garnish

YOGURT SAUCE

6. Add the yogurt, milk, and sugar into a small bowl and mix until smooth. Set aside.

PREPARATION

7. Scoop out a palmful of dough and lightly coat all sides with flour. Hold the dough in one palm and using your fingers of your other hand, pull the perimeter into the center. Repeat this motion all the way around.

8. While still holding the dough in your palm, flip the dough to the opposite side. Cup the top of the dough with your other hand and make a ball.

9. Press both sides of the dough into a shallow plate of flour to form a disc. With your palm and fingers, gently squeeze the perimeter of the dough to flatten it.

10. Place two pieces of dough on your work surface and, using a rolling pin, lightly roll the dough into circles the size of your opened hand.

11. Scoop a small palmful of the filling into the center of one dough circle, creating a little mound. Leave a perimeter around the edges, similar to a pizza crust.

12. Place another dough circle on top and crimp the edges with your fingertips, encasing the aloo filling.

13. Carefully roll the filled dough into a circle. Be sure to not add too much pressure to the paratha or you may risk squeezing the filling out of the dough. Keep your hands light and let the rolling pin do the work. The end product will look like a pancake with flecks of the filling showing through. Repeat steps 7 through 13 to create the remaining parathas.

14. Place the pan over medium-high heat until you see smoke. Carefully transfer the first aloo paratha into the heated pan and cover it with oil or ghee. Cook until the top turns light brown, about 1 minute. Flip and add more oil or ghee and cook for another 30 seconds to 2 minutes, periodically rotating with tongs to ensure even cooking and crispy and golden-brown exteriors.

STEP 2

STEP 9

STEP 12

STEP 13

Puri

What could be better than fried bread early in the morning? Commonly paired with chana, paya, and halwa puri, this puri is a family favorite and the perfect breakfast food. My family and I would go out for breakfast, often to a local Pakistani restaurant. I'd eat so many puris that I'd often find myself taking a long midday nap—these puris are very filling.

Yield: 4 puris
Prep time: 45 minutes
Cook time: 1 and a half minutes (30 seconds per puri)

EQUIPMENT

a large, deep, wide pot, like a
    karahi or a wok

rolling pin

INGREDIENTS

2 saucers of atta (page 23)

2 spoonfuls semolina flour

1 spoonful baking powder

olive oil

neutral oil, for deep frying

TIPS

* The first puri should be a test run; adjust the time and temperature accordingly.

* To test if the cooking oil is ready, you may either carefully drop a small piece of flattened dough into it and see if the dough bubbles or dip a wooden spoon or chopstick and see if small bubbles form around it. If so, the oil is ready.

1. In a medium mixing bowl, combine the atta, semolina flour, baking powder, and a drizzle of olive oil and mix well to combine. Fill a small jug or pitcher with water. Continue mixing dough, while periodically adding splashes of water as needed. The end product should be quite dense and similar to modeling clay.

2. Cover the bowl with a clean kitchen towel and set aside to rest at room temperature for 15 minutes.

3. Place the dough on a work surface and knead it with your palms and knuckles for a few minutes until smooth.

4. Grease your hands with olive oil and roll the dough into a log shape.

5. Cut the dough into five equal pieces. Shape each piece into a golf ball-sized dough ball.

6. Place the dough balls in an airtight container. Coat the dough-ball tops with olive oil. Cover the container and set aside for 20 minutes.

7. Add enough oil to cover the karahi or wok about a ¼ of the way up the sides with vegetable oil and set it over medium-high heat.

8. One at a time, place a dough ball on your work surface. With an oiled rolling pin, roll the dough into a thin circle. It should be thin enough to see through.

9. Carefully transfer the thin dough to the heated oil and press down with tongs or a slotted spoon, which will allow the puri to puff into a ball. Flip the puri, and cook until golden brown on both sides, about 30 seconds total (see Tips).

10. Remove the puri from the oil and place on a paper towel to remove excess oil.

11. Serve the puri immediately or transfer to a towel-lined plate and cover to keep warm while rolling and cooking the remaining dough. Pair with Chana or Paya (pages 91 and 84).

STEP 9

STEP 9

Garlic Naan

Naan might be the king of flatbreads. It's light and fluffy on the inside and crisp on the outside. I just love how it soaks up rich gravies. Growing up, whenever we went to a Pakistani restaurant, I'd always order extra naan to go because they tasted completely different than the ones we made at home. Restaurants use charcoal tandoor ovens, which are not very common in a home environment, unfortunately. In Pakistan, naan differs from city to city. Naan can be long and dense, oval or round, and crispy or soft. Naan is a blank canvas, so paint your picture!

Yield: 6–8 naans, depending how big you make them
Prep time: 1 hour 15 minutes
Cook time: 4 minutes

EQUIPMENT

rolling pin

food processor

GARLIC BUTTER

half bulb of garlic, cloves peeled

1 stick unsalted butter, room temperature

palmful of fresh cilantro leaves, roughly chopped

DOUGH

1 small spoonful instant yeast

pinch of granulated sugar

4 saucers of all-purpose flour, divided

pinch of salt

2 spoonfuls plain yogurt

1 egg

olive oil, for coating and cooking

GARLIC BUTTER

1. In a food processor, combine the garlic cloves, butter, and cilantro, pulsing until thoroughly mixed. Transfer to a bowl and set aside.

DOUGH

2. Fill a small jug or pitcher with room temperature water. In a small bowl, pour 2 seconds' worth of water from the jug and add the yeast and sugar. Stir to combine the ingredients and set bowl aside for 5 minutes.

3. To a large mixing bowl, add 3 saucers of flour, salt, yogurt, and egg, along with the yeast mixture, and using your hands, mix well to combine. Periodically pour a splash of water into the bowl. Continue kneading and mixing until a sticky dough is formed.

4. Keeping the dough in the bowl, evenly coat the top of the dough with olive oil, cover the bowl with a clean kitchen towel, and transfer it to the fridge for 1 hour or up to overnight to rest.

5. Remove the dough from the fridge and remove a palmful of the dough. Using the remaining saucer of flour, lightly coat all sides of the dough with it.

6. Hold the piece of dough in one palm and using the fingers of your other hand, pull the dough from the perimeter into the center and press. Repeat this motion all the way around.

7. Cup the dough in the palm of your hand and with your other hand, make a dough ball. Transfer the dough ball to a baking sheet. Repeat this process with the remaining dough (steps 4 to 6). Cover the dough balls with a clean kitchen towel and rest for 30 minutes at room temperature.

8. Preheat a skillet or sauté pan over medium-high heat. The pan is ready to cook with once it begins to smoke just a little.

9. Sprinkle your work surface with flour. Lightly press the dough ball into the flour, evenly coating both sides, and press to form a disc. With your fingers, gently press the perimeter of the dough and begin to flatten the ball.

10. Using a rolling pin, roll the dough into a circle, or if you have experience with making pizza, you may try shaping the dough by hand. The end product should be thin but not transparent and you should be able to easily hold it with your hands without it tearing apart.

11. Drizzle oil into the preheated pan, carefully add flattened dough, and cook until lightly golden brown; flip the naan and cook the other side until golden. Remove the naan from the pan and generously spread garlic butter on the top side.

12. Serve the naan immediately or transfer to a plate and cover with a clean kitchen towel to keep it warm while rolling out and cooking the remaining pieces dough.

STEP 3

STEP 3

STEP 3

STEP 6

TIPS

❋ You don't want to press the dough too hard when making it into a circle. You'll lose the light and fluffy texture of the dough and the naan will be tough.

❋ I tend to keep old cookie tins and fill them with flour (one for AP flour and one for atta) to use for easy coating when I'm making flatbreads.

Keema Naan

You can't go wrong with stuffed flatbread. Given naan is the king of flatbreads, having one stuffed with a spicy beef filling makes it a full-on meal. This isn't something that I make on a regular basis since I find it's more of a special treat. I'm sure to whip this up whenever there's a large gathering, and it's usually the first thing that runs out. The keema filling can also be eaten as a standalone dish, or over rice.

Yield: 6–8 naans, depending on how big you make them
Prep time: 1 hour 15 minutes
Cook time: 10 minutes

EQUIPMENT
tawa or any flat pan

rolling pin

DOUGH
1 small spoonful instant yeast

pinch of granulated sugar

4 saucer plates of all-purpose flour, divided

pinch of salt

2 spoonfuls plain yogurt

1 egg

olive oil

KEEMA
1 large handful or ½ lb (225g) of 80/20 ground beef

1 medium white onion, finely chopped

palmful of chopped fresh cilantro

3 green Thai chili peppers (or more if you like it spicy) (see Tips)

1 spoonful chili powder

½ spoonful ground cumin

½ spoonful ground coriander

1 spoonful salt

DOUGH

1. Fill a small jug or pitcher with room temperature water. In a small bowl, pour 2 seconds worth of water from the jug and add the yeast and sugar. Stir to combine the ingredients, and set the bowl aside for 5 minutes.

2. To a large mixing bowl, add 3 saucers of flour, salt, yogurt, and egg, along with the yeast mixture, and using your hands, mix well to combine. Periodically pour a splash of water into the bowl. Continue kneading and mixing until a sticky dough is formed into a shaggy ball.

3. Keeping the dough in the bowl, evenly coat the top of the dough with olive oil, cover the bowl with a clean kitchen towel, and transfer it to the fridge for 1 hour or up to overnight to rest.

4. Remove the dough from the fridge and remove a palmful of the dough. Using the remaining saucer of flour, lightly coat all sides of the dough with it.

5. Hold the piece of dough in one palm and using the fingers of your other hand, pull the dough from the perimeter into the center and press. Repeat this motion all the way around.

6. Cup the dough in the palm of your hand and with

your other hand, make a dough ball. Transfer the dough ball to a baking sheet. Repeat this process with the remaining dough (steps 4 to 6). Cover the dough balls with a clean kitchen towel and rest for 30 minutes at room temperature.

KEEMA

7. In a large bowl, add all ingredients and mix until thoroughly combined.

8. Preheat a large sauté or frying pan or wok over medium-high heat, add a small amount of neutral cooking oil, and carefully add the keema mixture.

9. Using a wooden spoon or heatproof spatula, break the meat into small bits and cook the keema until it begins to brown. Remove the pan from the heat when the meat is about 80% cooked, roughly 6 minutes.

PREPARATION

10. Using the remaining saucer of flour, lightly press the dough ball into the flour, evenly coating both sides and pressing to form a disc. With your fingers, gently press the perimeter of the dough and begin to flatten.

11. Using a rolling pin, roll the dough into a circle, or if you have experience with making pizza, you may try shaping the dough by hand. The end product should be thin but not transparent. Repeat with the remaining dough balls.

12. Scoop a palmful of the keema into the center of one of the dough circles, creating a little mound. Be sure to leave empty space around the perimeter, similar to a pizza crust. Gently place a second circle of dough on top and crimp the edges using your fingers.

13. Carefully pick up stuffed naan, and with your hands on either side of the roti, gently begin rotating it in your hands to stretching the dough, using a slow clapping motion.

14. Carefully roll the dough into a circle. Be sure to not add too much pressure or you may squeeze out the filling.

15. Preheat the tawa or pan over medium-high heat until it begins to smoke, add a small amount of neutral cooking oil, and carefully add the naan to the pan. Cook until the naan is golden brown, flip, and continue cooking until the opposite side is also golden.

16. Remove naan from the pan and enjoy immediately, or transfer it to a towel-lined plate and cover to keep it warm while cooking the remaining filled naans.

TIPS

＊ Green Thai chili peppers are spicy! Be cautious with how many you use. Try nibbling one to determine the heat and then add one or more according to your desired taste.

＊ Brush the cooked naan with melted butter immediately. Sprinkle your favorite garnish or seeds (e.g., sesame seeds) over the top of the naan before cooking.

STEP 10

STEP 10

STEP 11

STEP 11

STEP 12

STEP 12

STEP 13

CLASSICS

I grew up eating these dishes for lunch and dinner. You can think of "classics" as the main course. These are the dishes that everybody is waiting around for in the kitchen, while constantly asking the aunties how much longer it'll take until they can eat. Most of these classic dishes will have a key meat component, but there are also a few with only veggies. If you are looking to impress someone or trying to win that special someone's approval, and you nail one of these dishes, you'll be in their good books.

Ginger, Turmeric, and Garlic Paste

I like to call this the "Pakistani trinity." The combination of ginger, turmeric, and garlic is a staple in Pakistani cuisine. This blend of ingredients is incredibly aromatic, spicy, and earthy, and it provides the foundation for many Pakistani dishes. My mother learned this recipe from my grandmother when she was a little girl and has passed it to me. I hope you use and enjoy it as often as I do.

Yield: Roughly 10 spoonfuls
Prep time: 5 minutes

EQUIPMENT:
food processor

INGREDIENTS

2 handfuls garlic cloves, peeled

1 handful chopped ginger, (thumb-sized pieces)

1 handful chopped fresh turmeric root, (medium pieces)

1. In a food processor, combine the garlic, ginger, and turmeric and then pulse to coarsely blend the ingredients.

2. Slowly add water until the ingredients form a smooth paste.

3. Transfer to an airtight container and refrigerate the paste for up to 2 weeks, or freeze the paste in ice cube trays for easy storage and use. Frozen paste is good for up to 6 months.

TIPS

* Turmeric stains like crazy! It may be impossible to remove the stain from surfaces. Be careful to not get any on clothes, cutting boards, or knives that you care about. Wear gloves throughout the preparation process.

* Play with the ratios of the ingredients to make it your own! A little more of any one of the ingredients can transform the flavor profile of a dish!

* Mama commonly shapes the the paste into balls by taking out a heaping spoonful, squeezing out all the liquid, and forming them into little balls. These can then be transferred to a tray and frozen. It's then tossed in a Ziplock bag and left in the freezer until it's ready to be used.

Chicken Tikka

Whenever I go to a barbecue restaurant, I have a difficult time choosing between chicken or beef. I usually lean toward chicken and save beef for special occasions. You really can't go wrong with a spiced chicken on the grill.

Yield: 2–4 servings (as a starter or side)
Prep time: 60 minutes (up to overnight)
Cook time: 15 minutes

EQUIPMENT

2 metal or soaked bamboo skewers

heat-safe basting brush

INGREDIENTS

4 boneless chicken thighs, cubed

1 heaping spoonful chili powder

1 heaping spoonful Kashmiri red chili powder, optional (see Tip)

1 spoonful Garam Masala (page 20)

1 spoonful dried fenugreek leaves

½ spoonful ajwain (carom seeds)

1 heaping spoonful salt, or to taste

3 heaping spoonfuls yogurt

2 splashes white vinegar

2 spoonfuls Ginger, Turmeric, and Garlic Paste (page 60)

4 tablespoons unsalted butter, melted

> **TIP**
> When seasoning, a general rule is to ensure the ingredient is evenly coated. Sprinkle the spices over it to form an even layer on all sides. After it's cooked make a note if you would want more or less next time.

1. In a large mixing bowl, add chicken, chili powder, Kashmiri red chili powder, if using, garam masala, fenugreek leaves, carom seeds, salt, yogurt, vinegar, and Ginger, Turmeric, and Garlic Paste. Mix well to combine. Cover and transfer the bowl to the fridge to marinate for at least 1 hour or, preferably, overnight.

2. Remove the bowl from the fridge and place the chicken onto the skewers, evenly divided.

3. Preheat your grill to high. Turn off one side of the grill, or if using charcoal, move the briquettes to one side leaving half of the grill empty.

4. Place chicken skewers directly over the heat and sear on all sides, about 1 to 2 minutes per side.

5. Once the chicken is seared, liberally brush it with melted butter and transfer the skewers to indirect heat to finish the cooking process, about 7–10 minutes. Rotate the skewers frequently to ensure even cooking and brush with additional butter as needed.

6. Remove chicken from the grill and carefully slide Chicken Tikka pieces off the skewers and onto a platter. Serve alongside Garlic Naan (page 51) and Mint Chutney (page 122).

Chicken Karahi

In my experience, chicken karahi is a staple dish in most Pakistani homes and is commonly found on dinner tables a few times a month. For anyone new to Pakistani cuisine, I'd suggest starting with this recipe, a chicken curry of sorts. Karahi refers to a large, deep steel pan that's similar to a wok. Chefs and cooks use a karahi over high heat and continuously rotate food with heavy steel tongs. For us home cooks, any deep pan or wok works perfectly.

Yield: 4 servings
Prep time: 3 minutes
Cook time: 25 minutes

EQUIPMENT
karahi, wok, or another deep pan

INGREDIENTS
ghee or vegetable oil

4 bone-in chicken thighs and legs, chopped into chunks using a cleaver

2 spoonfuls of salt, or to taste

8 grinds freshly cracked black pepper

2 spoonfuls Ginger, Turmeric, and Garlic Paste (page 60)

2 large tomato, diced

6 green Thai chili peppers, thinly sliced on bias, for garnish (see Tip)

½ spoonful ground cinnamon

½ spoonful Garam Masala (page 20)

½ spoonful red pepper flakes

½ spoonful Kashmiri red chili powder

½ spoonful ground clove

3 spoonfuls plain yogurt

splash of heavy cream

chopped cilantro, for garnish

fresh ginger, peeled and thinly sliced, for garnish

1. Place a large pan over high heat and add enough ghee or oil to shallow fry. Add the chicken pieces to the oil and cook until light brown, about 3 to 5 minutes.

2. Season chicken with salt and pepper and then add the Ginger, Turmeric, and Garlic Paste, tomatoes, and Thai peppers (reserving some Thai peppers for topping). Reduce the temperature to medium-high heat, cover the pan, and cook for 10 minutes.

3. Add the cinnamon, garam masala, red pepper flakes, chili powder, and clove and then mix well. After a couple of minutes, add yogurt and heavy cream to the pan. Cook for 5 minutes. The end product should be a thin sauce that evenly coats the chicken.

4. Plate and garnish with the remaining Thai pepper, cilantro, and ginger. Enjoy with Roti (page 28 or Garlic Naan (page 50).

TIPS

✳ When adding spices to recipes, a general rule is to ensure the main ingredient is completely coated. When gauging the quantity of spices to add, look at your protein and estimate how many pinches or spoonfuls you'll need—and don't be afraid to make mistakes. Each time you prepare a recipe, estimating will become easier.

✳ Green Thai chili peppers are spicy! Be cautious with how many you use. Try nibbling one to determine the heat and then add one or more according to your desired taste.

Seekh Kabob

I'm often asked my favorite food. Although difficult to answer, kabobs in general are somewhere at the top of the list. And of all the different kinds, Seekh Kabob has to be my favorite. Growing up, I would go to Pakistani restaurants and not have to look at the menu because the only food I wanted was kabobs. Kabobs are great cooked in a tandoor, but the majority of us don't have one at home, so a grill will do just fine.

Yield: 4 servings
Prep time: 30 minutes
Cook time: 15 minutes

EQUIPMENT
fine-mesh sieve or cheesecloth

4 metal or soaked bamboo skewers

heatproof basting brush

INGREDIENTS
half bulb of garlic, cloves peeled

green Thai chili pepper, to taste (see Tips)

½ handful beef fat trimmings (see Tips)

1 medium onion, grated

2 large handfuls or 1lb (450g) 80/20 ground beef

1 spoonful chili powder

1 spoonful ground cumin

1 spoonful ground coriander

4 to 5 grinds of freshly ground black pepper

sea salt, to taste

4 spoonfuls melted butter

Mint Chutney, for serving (page 122)

1. Preheat your grill to high. Turn off one side of the grill, or if using charcoal, move the briquettes to one side leaving half of the grill empty.

2. In a food processor, add garlic cloves and Thai peppers, and pulse until finely chopped.

3. To the garlic-and-chili mixture, add beef fat and pulse until small, pebble-like pieces are formed.

4. Using your hands, press grated onion through a fine-mesh strainer or cheesecloth to remove excess water and set aside.

5. In a large bowl, combine ground beef, garlic-and-chili mixture, strained onion, chili powder, cumin, coriander, black pepper, and salt. Using your hands, mix the beef until it's a sticky consistency and the seasonings are well combined.

6. Line a baking sheet with foil or waxed paper. To form the kabobs, dip your hands into warm water to prevent the mixture from sticking, then scoop a palmful of the ground beef and shape it into a tight ball.

7. Using your hands, place one ball of beef around each skewer and gently squeeze lengthwise to form a cylinder, similar in shape to a hot dog. (If cooking in a pan on the stovetop, forgo the skewer

and form the meat into long cylinders without a skewer.) Place each prepared skewer on the baking sheet.

8. Begin by cooking the kabobs over direct heat. Sear the kebabs by placing skewers directly on the grill and cook, rotating every minute, until golden brown, about 4 minutes.

9. Once the kabobs are seared, liberally brush them with melted butter and place them over indirect heat to finish the cooking process, about 8 to 10 minutes. Rotate the kabobs frequently while cooking.

10. Carefully slide the cooked kabobs off the skewers while still warm and place on a platter. Serve alongside Garlic Naan (see page 50) and Mint Chutney (see page 122). Do NOT serve with ketchup!

TIPS

* Green Thai chili peppers are spicy! Be cautious with how many you use. Try nibbling one so you understand what you're dealing with and add according to your taste.

* When adding spices to recipes, a general rule is to ensure the main ingredient is completely coated. When gauging the quantity of spices to add look at your protein and estimate how many pinches or spoonfuls you'll need. Each time you prepare a recipe, estimating will become easier.

* To test kabobs for seasoning, make a mini kabob, around the size of your fingertip, and cook it on the stovetop until it's done. Adjust the seasoning if necessary.

Shami Kabob

The battle of kabobs! There are many different kinds, so choosing just one as my favorite is very difficult. Shami comes from the word shaam in Urdu, which loosely translates to "evening." Shami Kabob is the perfect dish for dinner and has a softer consistency when combined with lentils.

Yield: 4 servings
Prep time: 1 hour 5 minutes, plus 3 hours soak time
Cook time: 1 hour 5 minutes

INGREDIENTS

4 spoonfuls split chickpeas, soaked in water for 3 hours

1 handful or ½ lb (225g) 80/20 ground beef

1 heaping spoonful salt

4 grinds of freshly cracked black pepper

1 spoonful chili powder

½ spoonful cumin seeds

pinch of whole cloves

pinch of cardamom pods

½ cinnamon stick

2 spoonfuls Ginger, Turmeric, and Garlic Paste (page 60)

pinch of fresh mint leaves

palmful of chopped fresh cilantro

4 eggs, divided

ghee

TIP
Ensure the patties are tightly and compactly formed so they don't break apart while cooking. Searing the patties well forms a crust that helps hold the patty together.

1. In a pot, combine chickpeas, beef, salt, pepper, chili powder, cumin seeds, cloves, cardamom, cinnamon stick, and Ginger, Tumeric, and Garlic Paste and mix well.

2. Cover the meat with water, just about half a knuckle above the surface of the beef. Place the pot over medium heat. Simmer until all the water evaporates, about 1 hour. Check regularly to monitor the evaporation and avoid burning the meat. Remove from the heat and cool.

3. Transfer meat mixture to a food processor and add mint, cilantro, and 2 eggs. Pulse until smooth.

4. Evenly divide the mixture and form four hamburger-size patties. Place patties on a parchment paper–lined baking sheet and transfer the sheet to the fridge to firm for 1 hour.

5. Place a large pan over medium heat and add an even layer of ghee to cover the surface of the pan.

6. Whisk 2 eggs in a bowl and dip the patties into the scrambled eggs to fully coat each. Add the patties to the preheated pan and sear for 2 minutes on each side (see Tip). Remove the patties and enjoy immediately with naan and your choice of chutney.

Kofta

Many cultures seem to have their own version of a kofta (meatball); this is the Pakistani version. These meatballs are cooked in a masala (spice) sauce and are commonly eaten with naan. Growing up in Canada, I'd often see people enjoying the Italian classic spaghetti and meatballs. It looked so good that I'd ask my mother to cook spaghetti alongside kofta from time to time.

Yield: 4 servings
Prep time: 20 minutes
Cook time: 30 minutes

EQUIPMENT
blender

MASALA
1 medium onion, chopped

1 small tomato, chopped

1 spoonful Ginger, Turmeric, and Garlic Paste (page 60)

½ spoonful coriander seeds

4 green Thai chili peppers (see Tips)

½ spoonful ground clove

½ spoonful ground cinnamon

1 heaping spoonful chili powder

1 spoonful salt

MEATBALLS
2 large handfuls or 1lb (450g) 80/20 ground beef

½ spoonful chili powder

½ spoonful garam masala

½ spoonful cumin seeds

1 spoonful white poppy seeds

1 spoonful salt

palmful of chopped cilantro, plus extra for garnish

1 egg

vegetable oil

4 spoonfuls plain yogurt

1. To make the masala, in a blender, combine the onion, tomato, Ginger, Turmeric, and Garlic Paste, coriander seeds, Thai peppers, cloves, cinnamon, chili powder, and salt. Add enough water to create a pureé and blend until smooth. Transfer to a bowl and set aside.

2. To begin the meatballs, in a mixing bowl, combine beef, chili powder, garam masala, cumin seeds, poppy seeds, salt, cilantro, and egg. Mix well to combine. Using your hands, form the mixture into koftas—slightly larger than a golf ball is a good size, but it's up to you.

3. Place a pot over medium-high heat and evenly coat the bottom with neutral oil. (See Tips.) Add the prepared koftas and sear them on all sides until golden brown, about 1 to 2 minutes per side. Remove the koftas from the pan and set aside.

4. To the pan, add the masala mixture and scrape the residue from the bottom of the pan using a wooden spoon or heatproof spatula (deglaze). Cook the masala until aromatic, about 2 to 3 minutes.

5. Add koftas back to the pan and cook for another 10 minutes. Carefully stir the kofta to gently and evenly coat them with the masala.

6. Reduce the temperature to low, cook, covered for 5 minutes, then turn off the heat and add the yogurt. Mix, cover, and allow to sit for an additional 5 minutes.

7. To serve, transfer koftas to a plate and garnish with cilantro and enjoy with naan or spaghetti.

TIPS

✶ Green Thai chili peppers are spicy! Be cautious with how many you use. Try nibbling one to determine the heat and then add one or more according to your desired taste.

✶ The pot used should not be too large since the kofta should be submerged in the masala at least halfway up the meatballs.

✶ To test the kofta for seasoning, make a mini kofta, around the size of your fingertip, and cook it in the pan until it's done. Adjust the seasoning, if necessary.

Kerela

Similar to paya (trotters), people tend to love or hate karela (bitter melon). It took me many years to develop a taste for karela—after all, it is so bitter! But now that I'm older and my palate has matured, I've learned to appreciate how some ingredients pair with others, creating something magical. In this case, we're pairing karela with keema (minced meat).

Yield: 4 servings
Prep time: 30 minutes
Cook time: 25 minutes

EQUIPMENT
cooking or butcher's twine

INGREDIENTS
4 bitter melons

2 pinches of salt, divided

1 medium tomato, diced

1–4 green Thai chili peppers, diced (see Tips)

1 medium onion, diced

1 handful or ½ lb (225g) 80/20 ground beef

1 spoonful chili powder

½ spoonful Garam Masala (page 20)

ghee

1 spoonful Ginger, Turmeric, and Garlic Paste (see page 60)

1. Using a vegetable peeler, remove the rough outer layer of the bitter melons. Cut the bitter melons lengthwise, leaving one side uncut, so they open like a clam shell—do not cut through the entire melon. Remove and discard the seeds inside of the melons with a small spoon.

2. Place the bitter melons in a large bowl, cover them with water, add a large pinch of salt, and soak the melons for at least 15 minutes. This will help remove some of the bitter flavor. Drain the water.

3. Place the bitter melons in a large pot, add a good pinch of salt, and cover them with fresh water. Place the lid on the pot and bring the water to a boil over high heat. Reduce the heat to medium and simmer for 10 minutes or until the melons are fork-tender. Remove melons from the water and drain on a paper towel–lined baking sheet.

4. In a mixing bowl, combine tomato, Thai peppers, onion, ground beef, chili powder, and garam masala and mix well.

5. Place a large pan over medium-high heat, add ghee to the pan to coat the surface and then add the ground beef mixture. Cook the beef, breaking it into small pieces. After approximately 5 minutes, add Ginger, Turmeric, and Garlic Paste to the meat, and

cook for another 5 to 10 minutes or until meat is cooked through. Remove from heat and set aside.

6. Place the melons on a plate and open them up to expose the center. Scoop beef mixture into the center of the melons and then close them to seal in the beef. Using butcher's twine, tie the bitter melon shut in four or five spots along the length of the melon. Set aside.

7. Place a large pan over high heat and add ghee to evenly coat the bottom. Add the melons and sear them on all sides until golden brown, about 2 to 3 minutes per side.

8. Remove the melons from the pan and transfer to a plate, remove the strings, and enjoy immediately with your favorite chutney.

TIPS

❊ This dish can also be made by slicing the bitter melons after boiling them and then cooking them with the ground beef. It's common to eat this style of kerela with roti or paratha.

❊ Green Thai chili peppers are spicy! Be cautious with how many you use. Try nibbling one to determine the heat and then add one or more according to your desired taste.

Beef Nihari

I love slow-cooked beef, it's so tender, and just thinking about it makes me drool. This meat is cooked "low and slow," at a low temperature for a long period of time, creating a rich, flavorful stock. Nihari with naan, to help soak up all that stock, is definitely in my top five meals.

Yield: 6 servings
Prep time: 10 minutes
Cook time: 60 minutes if using a pressure cooker or 5½ hours on the stove

---

EQUIPMENT
blender

large Dutch oven with a lid (big enough to hold the meat comfortably) or a pressure cooker

INGREDIENTS
1 spoonful chili powder

2 bay leaves

1 spoonful cardamom pods

1 spoonful cumin seeds

½ spoonful fennel seeds

pinch of whole cloves

1 spoonful Kashmiri red chili powder (or your favorite chili powder)

1 spoonful black peppercorns

3 spoonfuls ghee, divided

2 handful or 1lb (453g) bone-in chuck round

2 handfuls or 2lbs (900g) shank roast (with a marrow bone)

2 spoonfuls Ginger, Turmeric, and Garlic Paste (see page 60)

2 small onions, thinly sliced

2 spoonfuls salt or to taste

4 spoonfuls atta (see page 23)

1. In a blender, combine the chili powder, bay leaves, cardamom pods, cumin seeds, fennel seeds, cloves, Kashmiri red chili powder, and peppercorns, and pulse to make a powdered spice blend. Transfer powder to a bowl and set aside.

2. Heat a large Dutch oven or pressure cooker to medium-high heat. Add 2 spoonfuls of ghee to the cooking surface to coat the pot and then add all the meat and sear the pieces on all sides until lightly browned, about 2 minutes per side. Remove the meat from the pot and set aside.

3. To the pot, add Ginger, Turmeric, and Garlic Paste and stir for a couple of minutes until aromatic.

4. Add onions to the pot and stir until they are light brown in color. Add the meat back to the pot and season it with salt and the spice blend and mix well, reserving a bit of the spice blend for later use.

5. Cover the meat with water, mix the ingredients into the water, and place the lid on the pot. Cook over low heat for about 5 hours, stirring the broth every hour. (If using a pressure cooker, this can be cooked on high in about 45 minutes.) Meat should be fork-tender and falling off the bone.

6. In a bowl, combine flour with a little water to create a loose paste. Add the flour mixture to the pot,

chopped cilantro, for garnish

chopped green Thai chili pepper, for garnish

fresh ginger, peeled and sliced into matchsticks, for garnish

squeeze of lemon juice

cover, and continue cooking over low heat for an additional 10 minutes or until the sauce is thickened.

7. In a small separate pan, add the remaining spoonful of ghee and remaining spice blend. Cook over medium heat until aromatic, about 1 minute, and add this mixture to the pot and mix it in.

8. To serve, place one piece of beef in a bowl with the gravy and garnish the nihari with a squeeze of lemon juice, cilantro, green Thai chili peppers, and sliced ginger.

TIP
This dish is commonly made with beef, but you can also use lamb shanks or chicken legs.

Baingan Gosht

Eggplant (baingan) is probably my favorite vegetable, and when combined with tender lamb (gosht) or goat, this dish is an absolute win-win. I prefer using baby eggplants for this dish, as they offer a nicer presentation.

Yield: 4 servings
Prep time: 15 minutes
Cook time: 40 minutes in a pressure cooker or about 85 minutes on the stove

---

EQUIPMENT
pressure cooker, optional

BAINGAN
12 mini eggplants

neutral oil

1 spoonful fenugreek seeds

1 spoonful black caraway seeds

1 spoonful chili powder

1 spoonful Garam Masala
    (page 20)

medium bowl of yogurt

squeeze of lemon juice

GOSHT
neutral oil

1 large onion, thinly sliced

2 large handfuls or 1lb (450g)
    bone-in lamb or goat meat
    (shoulder or leg) cut into
    medium cubes using a
    cleaver

2 spoonfuls salt, or to taste

2 small tomatoes, finely chopped

1 heaping spoonful Ginger,
    Turmeric, and Garlic Paste
    (page 60)

Chopped cilantro, for garnish

BAINGAN

1. Slice eggplants lengthwise from the bottom toward the stem, leaving the stem intact.

2. Place a large pan with a lid over medium-high heat. Add oil to evenly coat the bottom of the pan and then add the eggplant halves. Sear eggplant on all sides until golden brown, about 3 to 4 minutes.

3. To the pan, add fenugreek seeds, caraway seeds, chili powder, garam masala, yogurt, lemon juice, and enough water to cover the bottom of the pan. Mix well, cover, and cook over low-medium heat for 10 minutes. Remove from heat and set aside.

GOSHT

4. Preheat a large pot or pressure cooker over medium heat. Add oil and onions to the pot and cook the onions until they are translucent but not browning, about 5 minutes. Transfer onion to a plate and set aside.

5. Increase heat to high, add the meat to the pot, and quickly sear on all sides until golden brown.

6. Season the meat cubes with salt and then add the cooked onions, tomatoes, and Ginger, Turmeric and Garlic Paste to the pot and mix well.

7. Cover the meat with water until about three-quarters submerged and then bring to a simmer. Reduce the

heat to low, cover, and cook for 45 to 60 minutes or until the meat is fork-tender and tears apart easily. If using a pressure cooker, this takes roughly 15 minutes.

8. Add the eggplant to the meat and mix well. Bring the mixture to a slow simmer over medium heat, cover, and continue simmering for 5 minutes.

9. To serve, spoon equal portions of the eggplant and gosht mixture with some broth into a bowl and garnish with cilantro. Enjoy!

TIP
When buying gosht from the market, always ask the butcher for bone marrow for next-level flavor.

TIP
Korma is commonly made with a variety of meats. Feel free to substitute the goat with chicken or lamb.

Korma

Korma is a great introductory dish. Think of it as a stew—in this case, goat. It's braised in spices and mixed with yogurt to give it a rich and creamy sauce. If you enjoy korma and want to try something spicier, check out Chicken Karahi (see page 64).

Yield: 4 servings
Prep time: 3 minutes
Cook time: 65 minutes on the stovetop or 35 minutes in a pressure cooker

EQUIPMENT
large stock pot or pressure cooker

INGREDIENTS
1 large spoonful ghee

1 large white onion, thinly sliced

2 spoonfuls Ginger, Turmeric, and Garlic Paste (page 60)

2 handfuls or 1lb (450g) bone-in goat meat (shoulder or leg), chopped into chunks using a cleaver

½ spoonful cumin seeds

½ cinnamon stick

pinch of green cardamom pods

pinch of whole cloves

pinch of black cardamom pods

½ spoonful black peppercorns

2 spoonfuls chili powder

2 spoonfuls salt, or to taste

small bowl of plain yogurt

squeeze of lemon juice

chopped cilantro, for garnish

fresh ginger, peeled and thinly sliced, for garnish

1. Place a large pot over medium-high heat, add ghee and onions, and cook until the onions are golden brown, about 5 minutes. Transfer onions to a plate and set aside.

2. To the pot, add Ginger, Turmeric, and Garlic Paste and stir until aromatic, about 2 minutes.

3. Add meat to the pot and sear it on all sides until golden brown, about 2 minutes per side.

4. Add cumin seeds, cinnamon stick, green cardamom pods, cloves, black cardamom pods, peppercorns, chili powder, and salt and mix well. Cook until the spices are toasted and aromatic, about 2 minutes.

5. Add yogurt to the pot, and add water, just enough that the top of the meat is still visible. Bring mixture to a simmer and cook until meat is fork-tender, about 45 minutes. (If using a pressure cooker, this takes about 15 minutes.) Once the meat is tender, add the cooked onions and lemon juice to the pot, cover, reduce the heat to low, and cook for an additional 5 minutes.

6. Serve korma on a plate and garnish it with cilantro and ginger. Enjoy with Roti (see page 28) or Paratha (see page 38).

Haleem

Another one of my favorite dishes, haleem, is a thick and hearty meat and lentil stew. It's great in the winter and epitomizes comfort food. I loved this dish as a child and remember eating it by the spoonful whenever I finished my naan. On a recent trip to Pakistan, I visited my mother's home city, Karachi, specifically to try their haleem. My mom's is way better.

Yield: 5 servings
Prep time: 5 minutes
Cook time: 2 hours on the stove or 45 minutes in a pressure cooker

---

EQUIPMENT
lidded stock pot or pressure cooker

hand blender

INGREDIENTS
4 spoonfuls each yellow, red, and urad lentils, soaked in water overnight

4 spoonfuls split chickpeas, soaked in water overnight

4 spoonfuls pearled wheat, soaked in water overnight

ghee

3 spoonfuls Ginger, Turmeric, and Garlic paste (page 60)

2 handfuls or 1 lb (450g) boneless beef shanks, cut into chunks

1 spoonful salt, or to taste

1 spoonful chili powder

1 spoonful Garam Masala (page 20)

1 spoonful cumin seeds

chopped fresh cilantro, for garnish

Sliced green Thai chili pepper, for garnish (see Tips)

thinly sliced ginger, for garnish

Crispy fried onions, for garnish

lemon wedges, for garnish

1. Strain the lentils, chickpeas, and pearled wheat and set aside.

2. Warm a large pot over medium heat and add enough ghee to cover the bottom of the pot. Add the Ginger, Turmeric, and Garlic paste and stir until aromatic, about 2 minutes.

3. Add the beef and sear on all sides, about 2 minutes per side. Add the salt, chili powder, garam masala, and cumin seeds and mix well.

4. Add the lentils, chickpeas, and pearled wheat into the pot and mix well.

5. Cover the ingredients with water until submerged, or up to your first knuckle when touching the beef.

6. Bring to a simmer and cook over medium-low heat until the meat is tender, about two hours (or a bit longer). If using a pressure cooker, about 30 minutes. The meat should be falling apart.

7. With your hand blender, pulse everything until a thick, smooth consistency is formed.

8. Serve in a deep plate. Garnish with cilantro, green chilis, sliced ginger, crumbled fried onions, and a squeeze of lemon juice. Enjoy with Garlic Naan (page 50).

TIPS

✳ If the mixture is too liquidy once the beef is cooked, remove the lid and continue simmering until you achieve the desired consistency. Don't forget to stir occasionally.

✳ After blending, remember to taste for seasoning and adjust accordingly.

✳ Green Thai chili peppers are spicy! Be cautious with how many you use. Try nibbling one to determine the heat and then add one or more according to your desired taste.

Daal Gosht

Daal gosht has incredible mouthfeel with tender goat meat and lentils in every bite. Daal (lentils) adds so much texture to this dish, which sets it apart from most gosht dishes. This dish was a staple in my home when growing up.

Yield: 4 servings
Prep time: 5 minutes
Cook time: 30 minutes in a pressure cooker or 60 minutes without one

---

EQUIPMENT
pressure cooker, optional

INGREDIENTS
ghee

1 medium onion, thinly sliced

2 spoonfuls Ginger, Turmeric, and Garlic Paste (page 60)

2 pounds (900g) (about 4 handfuls) bone-in goat shoulder and leg, cut into medium chunks using a cleaver

½ spoonful coriander seeds

1 spoonful chili powder

½ spoonful black peppercorns

½ cinnamon stick

pinch of cumin seeds

pinch of ground coriander

pinch of dried or fresh curry leaves

4 spoonfuls of split chickpeas, soaked for one hour at least and then drained (see Tips)

2 heaping spoonfuls salt or to taste

1 medium tomato, roughly chopped

sliced green Thai chili peppers, to taste (see Tips)

chopped cilantro, for garnish

1. In a large pot over medium heat, add ghee, onions, and Ginger, Turmeric, and Garlic Paste. Cook until onions are translucent, about 3 to 4 minutes.

2. Add goat meat, coriander seeds, chili powder, peppercorns, cinnamon stick, cumin seeds, ground coriander, curry leaves, and salt to the pot, and cover ingredients to about halfway with water. Bring the water to a simmer and then reduce the heat to medium-low. Cook until the meat is fork-tender and easily tears apart, about 45 minutes. If using a pressure cooker, this takes about 10 to 15 minutes.

3. In another pot, add soaked and drained split chickpeas and cover with fresh water until submersed by about a knuckle's width. Bring water to a simmer over medium-low heat and cook chickpeas until tender, about 30 minutes. If using a pressure cooker, this takes about 10 minutes.

4. To the goat meat mixture, add chopped tomato and Thai peppers and then mix well to combine. Bring gosht to a simmer and cook for 5 additional minutes. Add cooked split chickpeas to the gosht and mix. Simmer over low heat for another 5 minutes. Garnish with cilantro and serve.

Paya

Trotters are the feet of animals, for this recipe cow or lamb. In my experience, there is no grey area: people either love or hate them. Growing up, I hated trotters with their gelatinous, sticky texture that leaves a residue on your fingers, all were a turn-off for me. As I got older and my palate developed, I came to absolutely love them!

Yield: 4 servings
Prep time: 5 minutes
Cook time: 50 minutes in a pressure cooker or 3 hours on the stove

EQUIPMENT
large Dutch oven, stock pot, or
    pressure cooker

INGREDIENTS
ghee

1 pound (450g) cow or lamb
    trotters (roughly 7 pieces)

1 large onion, thinly sliced

2 spoonfuls Ginger, Turmeric, and
    Garlic Paste (page 60)

½ spoonful black peppercorns

pinch of green cardamom pods

pinch of black cardamom pods

½ spoonful cumin seeds

½ spoonful coriander seeds

1 spoonful Garam Masala (page 20)

pinch of whole cloves

1 spoonful chili powder

2 spoonfuls salt or to taste

chopped cilantro, for garnish

fresh ginger, peeled and thinly
    sliced, for garnish

1. Place a large pot or pressure cooker over medium-high heat.

2. Once the pot is hot, add ghee to the pot to coat it and then add the trotters to the pot and sear them on all sides until golden brown, about 2 minutes per side. Remove trotters from the pot and set aside.

3. Add the onion, Ginger, Turmeric, and Garlic Paste, peppercorns, green and black cardamom pods, cumin, coriander, garam masala, cloves, and salt to the pot. Stir often, cooking until the spices become aromatic, about 2 minutes.

4. Add trotters to the pot and cover them with water so the trotters are completely submerged.

5. Bring the water to a simmer and then reduce the heat to low and cook until the trotters are fork-tender, about 3 hours. If using a pressure cooker, cook for about 45 minutes on medium heat until fork-tender.

6. To serve, place 1 or 2 trotters and some of the broth into a bowl. Garnish with cilantro and ginger. Enjoy with naan.

TIP
Remember to taste your broth and adjust your seasonings to your taste before serving.

TIP

✳ Paneer is optional and can be removed or even replaced with tofu to make it vegan.

MAKE IT YOUR OWN

✳ There are many different types of saag, feel free to switch up the greens—for example broccoli rabe, kale, or collards.

✳ Green Thai chili peppers are spicy! Be cautious with how many you use. Try nibbling one so you understand what you're dealing with and add according to your taste.

Saag

All cultures have their version of slow-cooked greens. These are cooked mustard greens, Pakistani style. Saag is one of those dishes that replaces meat easily for a tasty, filling meal. When I first visited my father's town of Chakwal, Pakistan, I was blown away with the variety of saag his family fed us. In our home, we rarely ate raw greens; most are slow cooked with a soft texture.

Yield: 4 servings
Prep time: 10 minutes
Cook time: 2 hours on the stove or 45 minutes in a pressure cooker

---

EQUIPMENT NEEDED
lidded stock pot or pressure
    cooker
hand blender, optional

INGREDIENTS
12 handfuls mustard greens,
    roughly chopped

1 heaping spoonful salt, or to taste

1 spoonful chili powder

1 spoonful ground cumin

1 spoonful ground coriander

2 spoonfuls Ginger, Turmeric, and
    Garlic Paste (page 60)

green Thai chili peppers, to taste,
    roughly chopped (see Tips)

4 spoonfuls atta (page 23)

1 large onion, thinly sliced

spoonful of mustard oil

pinch of cumin seeds

1 handful paneer, cubed,
    for garnish

handful raw red onion slices,
    for garnish

1. In a large pot, add the mustard greens, salt, chili powder, ground cumin and coriander, Ginger, Turmeric, and Garlic Paste, and the green Thai chili peppers and enough water to fully cover ingredients. Bring to a simmer over medium-low heat, stirring every 20 minutes, until the liquid has evaporated, about 2 hours. If using a pressure cooker, about 45 minutes.

2. Add the flour and, using a large spoon or masher, mash the greens to achieve a smoother consistency. Alternatively, you can use a hand blender and pulse until a thick consistency is achieved.

3. Warm a large sauté pan over medium heat. Add the mustard oil and onions and cook, stirring often, until caramelized and golden brown, about 5 minutes. Add the cumin seeds and continue cooking until aromatic, about 2 minutes. Remove from the pan and set aside.

4. In the same pan add more oil and cubed paneer and sear on all sides until golden brown, about 30 seconds per side. Transfer to a plate and set aside.

5. To serve, place saag in a deep dish and garnish with pieces of paneer (if desired) and onions and enjoy with Roti (see page 28) or Paratha (see page 38).

Bhindi

Growing up, I really didn't have much of an appreciation for bhindi (okra). It has a strange, slimy texture. But as with many of the dishes in this book, my palate developed, and I grew to appreciate the texture and flavor of bhindi. If you've never tried okra before, this is a great recipe to introduce you to it.

Yield: 4 servings
Prep time: 5 minutes
Cook time: 15 minutes

INGREDIENTS

olive oil, divided

1 spoonful Ginger, Turmeric, and Garlic Paste (page 60)

1 large onion, thinly sliced and divided

1 medium tomato, diced

2 handfuls fresh okra, stemmed and roughly chopped

green Thai chili pepper, to taste, chopped (see Tips)

½ cinnamon stick

½ spoonful cumin seeds

1 spoonful chili powder

1 heaping spoonful salt or to taste

squeeze of fresh lemon juice

1. Place a medium saucepan over medium heat and add enough olive oil to evenly coat the pan. Add Ginger, Turmeric, and Garlic Paste and cook until aromatic, about 2 minutes.

2. Add most of the sliced onions (reserve a large pinch of onion slices for use later) and diced tomatoes, and cook until the onions are slightly brown, about 3 minutes. Add okra to the pan, increase the heat to medium-high, and stir until okra has a bit of color, about 3 minutes.

3. Add Thai peppers, cinnamon stick, cumin seed, chili powder, and salt. Mix well and cook until the spices are aromatic, about 2 minutes.

4. Reduce the heat to low. To the pan, add another drizzle of olive oil and the remaining sliced raw onions, cover the pan, and cook the onions for 5 minutes.

5. Remove the lid, squeeze lemon juice over the top, and mix well.

6. Enjoy immediately with Roti (page 28).

TIPS

* Oil will prevent the okra from sticking to the pan. If you find the okra is sticking, add more oil as needed.

* Green Thai chili peppers are spicy! Be cautious with how many you use. Try nibbling one to determine the heat and then add one or more according to your desired taste.

TIP

When I was in Lahore, Pakistan, I saw a chef add chicken legs to the pot and cook everything in chicken broth instead of water. That was probably the best chana I've ever had. This is supposed to be a vegetarian dish but feel free to get that extra protein in there!

Chana

Chana is a classic Pakistani breakfast dish—it's spicy, hearty, and quite addicting. One of the best chana I ever ate was in Lahore, Pakistan. Lines start very early in the morning for breakfast, as early as 4:00 a.m., so it was quite the sight to see. You know the food is amazing when people are willing to sacrifice their sleep just to line up for it.

Yield: 4 servings
Prep time: 5 minutes
Cook time: 25 minutes

INGREDIENTS

2 handfuls dried chickpeas, soaked overnight in water with a pinch of baking soda

1 large onion, finely chopped

1 medium potato, peeled and finely chopped

1 spoonful salt, or to taste

½ spoonful cumin seeds

½ cinnamon stick

½ spoonful chili powder

pinch of black caraway seeds

pinch of white sesame seeds

1 small tomato, diced

pinch of dried or fresh curry leaves

olive oil

palmful of chopped fresh cilantro

squeeze of fresh lemon juice

1. Strain chickpeas.

2. In a large saucepan, add chickpeas, onion, potato, salt, cumin seeds, cinnamon stick, chili powder, black caraway seeds, white sesame seeds, tomato, and curry leaves. Cover all ingredients with water, until it's about ½ a knuckle above the surface of the ingredients.

3. Cover the pot, bring the water to a simmer over medium heat, and cook the potatoes about 20 minutes, or until the water has evaporated and the potatoes are fork-tender.

4. Uncover the pot and drizzle olive oil over the top and mix well.

5. To serve, ladle some chana in a bowl and garnish with cilantro and lemon juice. Enjoy with Puri (page 46), Roti (page 28), or Paratha (page 38).

Aloo Gobi

Cauliflower is an underrated vegetable. Other than aloo gobi and Korean fried cauliflower (my favorite), I rarely see it prepared in a way I would actually enjoy it. I absolutely love how the cauliflower and potatoes absorb all that wonderful gravy. In my opinion, this is the perfect vegan dish.

Yield: 4 servings
Prep time: 5 minutes
Cook time: 35 minutes

INGREDIENTS

ghee

1 large onion, thinly sliced

1 spoon Ginger, Turmeric, and Garlic Paste (page 60)

2 small tomatoes, roughly chopped

1 heaping spoonful salt or to taste

1 spoonful chili powder

½ spoonful coriander seeds

½ spoonful cumin seeds

½ spoonful black caraway seeds

pinch of black peppercorns

green Thai chili peppers, to taste, chopped (see Tips)

½ cinnamon stick

1 head cauliflower, broken into florets

4 baby potatoes, cut in halves

palmful of chopped cilantro, for garnish

1. Place a large pan over medium-high heat. Add ghee and onions, as well as the Ginger, Turmeric, and Garlic Paste. Cook until aromatic and the onions begin to "sweat," about 2 minutes.

2. Add tomatoes, salt, chili powder, coriander seeds, cumin seeds, black caraway seeds, black peppercorns, Thai peppers, and cinnamon stick, and mix well. Continue cooking until spices become aromatic, about 2 minutes.

3. Add cauliflower and potatoes to the pot and mix well (see Tips). Add a mug of water to the pot, cover, and cook over medium heat until potatoes are fork-tender, about 25 minutes. Check about halfway through cooking and add a splash or two of water if needed.

4. To serve, ladle Aloo Gobi into a bowl and garnish with cilantro; enjoy immediately with Roti (page 28).

TIPS

✽ You don't want the cauliflower to be completely mushy, so be careful not to overcook it. To avoid this, you can try cooking the potatoes first and once they are almost fork-tender you can then add the cauliflower to the pot and finish the cooking process for the potatoes.

✽ Green Thai chili peppers are spicy! Be cautious with how many you use. Try nibbling one to determine the heat and then add one or more according to your desired taste.

TIPS

✴ Be careful not to mix the turnips and spinach too much as you want it to be a bit chunky. You don't want this to become smooth like mashed potatoes.

✴ Green Thai chili peppers are spicy! Be cautious with how many you use. Try nibbling one to determine the heat and then add one or more according to your desired taste.

Shaljam Palak

Other than pickled turnips in my shawarma and shaljam (turnips), I don't recall eating shaljam as a kid. Like cauliflower, turnips are underrated, and I've grown to love them. I have yet to try a tastier dish with turnips as the main ingredient.

Yield: 4 servings
Prep time: 7 minutes
Cook time: 35 minutes

EQUIPMENT
potato masher

INGREDIENTS
4 white turnips, peeled and roughly chopped

4–6 handfuls fresh spinach, roughly chopped

ghee

1 spoonful cumin seeds

sliced green Thai chili peppers to taste

2 medium tomatoes, roughly chopped

1 spoonful Ginger, Turmeric, and Garlic Paste (see page 60)

1 spoonful chili powder

1 heaping spoonful salt

2 spoonfuls plain yogurt

crispy fried onions, for garnish

1. Pour water into a pot, about 2–3 knuckles high when touching the bottom of the pan. Add turnips and spinach to the pot, cover, and cook over medium heat until the turnips are fork-tender, about 20 minutes.

2. Remove the pot from the heat and transfer mixture to a blender or use an immersion hand blender, leaving the mixture in the pot. Pulse just enough so it remains a thick and chunky texture. Set it aside.

3. Get another pot on the stove and over medium heat, add ghee, cumin seeds, Thai peppers, tomatoes, Ginger, Turmeric, and Garlic Paste, chili powder, salt, and yogurt and mix well. Continue cooking until spices are aromatic, about 2 to 3 minutes.

4. Add the turnip-and-spinach mixture into the new pot and mix well with the other ingredients. Cover and simmer for 10 minutes over medium heat.

5. Serve in bowls or on plates with a garnish of crispy onion straws. Enjoy with Roti (page 28).

Daal

Ask any desi kid if they like daal (lentils) and the chances are they don't. This very simple dish was made so often by my mother, it was tough for me to love. But now that I'm older, I absolutely love it and understand why it was made so often as a kid—it's comfort food that pairs with rice and roti, it's so versatile.

Yield: 4 servings
Prep time: 5 minutes
Cook time: 1½ hours on the stove or 40 minutes in a pressure cooker

---

EQUIPMENT
pressure cooker or lidded pot

INGREDIENTS
1 Green Thai chili pepper, or more, finely chopped (see Tips)

1 small tomato, diced

2 spoonfuls Ginger, Turmeric, and Garlic Paste (page 60)

1 spoonful chili powder

pinch of whole cloves

¼ mug of orange lentils (soaked in water for 2 hours)

¼ mug split chickpeas (soaked in water for 2 hours)

1 medium onion, sliced

1 heaping spoonful salt

ghee

1 spoonful cumin seeds

palmful of chopped cilantro

1. In a large pot combine the chili pepper, tomato, Ginger, Turmeric, and Garlic Paste, chili powder, cloves, and soaked lentils.

2. Cover with water just enough so that the water level reaches your first knuckle above the lentils. Cover the pot and bring to a simmer over medium-low heat, stirring every 30 minutes until the lentils break down and a smooth, thick texture is formed, about 1½ hours. If using a pressure cooker, about 40 minutes. While the daal is cooking, warm another pan over medium heat and add enough ghee to cover the entire bottom of the pan. Add the onions and cumin seeds and cook until onions are golden brown, about 5 minutes. Combine the daal with the onions and mix well to combine.

3. Serve immediately garnish with cilantro. Enjoy with either rice or Roti (page 28) and pickled veggies.

TIP
* When making daal, you don't have to be too precise with the water measurement, you can always adjust, adding more as you go.

MAKE IT YOUR OWN
* Feel free to use other types of lentils. Another common dish is called Daal Makhni, which has brown lentils and kidney beans and lots of butter.

TIPS

* To save time, lentils can be easily soaked overnight in your refrigerator.

* Green Thai chili peppers are spicy! Be cautious with how many you use. Try nibbling one to determine the heat and then add one or more according to your desired taste.

Mash ki Daal

Mash ki Daal is made with split white lentils and differs from the typical daal you've tried previously. This daal has an amazing chunky texture and is a great departure from the smoother consistency you may be used to. If you love lentils, as I do, this is a great way to mix it up and play with different methods of preparing them.

Yield: 4 servings
Prep time: 5 minutes
Cook time: 90 minutes

INGREDIENTS

1 mug of dried split white lentils, soaked in water for at least 3 hours (see Tips)

½ spoonful chili powder

½ spoonful black peppercorns

1 spoonful Ginger, Turmeric, and Garlic Paste (page 60)

½ cinnamon stick

½ spoonful black caraway seeds

1 heaping spoonful salt

ghee

1 medium onion, thinly sliced

sliced green Thai chili peppers, to taste (see Tips)

½ spoonful cumin seeds

palmful of chopped fresh cilantro, for garnish

1 or 2 radishes, thinly sliced, for garnish

1. Drain the lentils.

2. In a medium pot, add drained lentils, chili powder, black peppercorns, Ginger, Turmeric, and Garlic Paste, cinnamon stick, black caraway seeds, and salt and mix well to combine. Cover the ingredients with water up to your first knuckle. Don't worry, a little water more or less will not affect the recipe.

3. Bring the mixture to a simmer over medium heat, skimming the impurities (the foamy stuff floating to the top) and discarding them occasionally. Continue cooking until all the water has evaporated. Taste to ensure the lentils are soft and cooked. If lentils require additional cooking time, add more water, and continue cooking until you achieve the desired consistency, about 30 minutes.

4. Place a sauté pan over medium heat and cover the bottom of the pan with ghee. Add onion and sauté until golden brown and caramelized, about 5 minutes. Add green Thai pepper and cumin seeds and cook until the cumin seeds are aromatic, about 2 minutes.

5. Add the caramelized onions to lentils and mix well to combine.

6. Serve immediately, garnished with cilantro and radish. Enjoy with Roti (page 28).

Basmati Rice

Basmati is the king of rice and is the only rice we use in the Bhatti home. It is a long-grain rice and becomes light and fluffy when cooked perfectly. Without basmati rice, most meals would just feel incomplete. Cooking the perfect pot of rice takes practice and determination. It will take some time, but it's worth it.

Yield: 3 servings
Prep time: 35 minutes
Cook time: 10 to 15 minutes

INGREDIENTS

1 mug uncooked basmati rice

1 spoonful salt

pinch of cumin seeds

pinch of cloves

spoonful of melted butter

TIPS

* When washing the rice, be gentle with the grains so they don't break apart. They break quite easily.

* Use a large pot and lots of water to cook the rice in so the rice has more room to swirl around and there's less chance of it forming lumps (similar to how one may cook pasta).

* This recipe is your white canvas—make it your own! Substitute chicken or beef stock for water when cooking the rice. Add cooked chickpeas or green peas—or even drizzle saffron water with lots of dried dill—to the rice right before serving it.

1. Pour the rice into a mixing bowl and cover with cold water. Using your hands, gently swirl the rice to release the starch—the water will resemble milk (see Tips). Strain the rice and repeat the rinsing, swirling, and straining process until the water is clear. Submerge the rice one last time in cold water and let it sit for 30 minutes.

2. Strain the rice and place it in a large pot with plenty of water (see Tips). Add salt, cumin seeds, and cloves. bring the rice to a boil over high heat until al dente, about 7 to 10 minutes. Do a taste-test to ensure that the rice is not crunchy, but still has a bite to it.

3. Carefully pour the rice into a fine-mesh strainer placed over the sink and allow the water to drain. Then return the rice to the original pot. Add melted butter to the rice, cover the pot, and place it over very low heat, allowing the rice to steam for 5 minutes.

4. Uncover and lightly fluff the rice with a fork. You should be able to separate each grain individually. Serve immediately with your favorite meal.

TIPS

* Most lentils and beans have alternative names. The black split gram lentils used in this recipe are also known as "Urad black split dal" or "split black maitpe beans." Keep your phone handy to search what's offered at your local grocery store.

* Given the consistency of Khichdi is mushy, you don't have to worry about overcooking it because that's generally what's needed. To ensure nothing is crunchy, periodically taste test to see if the rice and lentils are soft and ready to serve.

* Green Thai chili peppers are spicy! Be cautious with how many you use. Try nibbling one to determine the heat and then add one or more according to your desired taste.

Khichdi

Khichdi is loved by everyone, from babies to adults. It's a dish of rice and lentils cooked with aromatic spices until they've reached a soft and smooth consistency—perfect food for toddlers since it doesn't require chewing. When I visited the city of Peshawar, customers would huddle around a man sitting in front of the biggest pot I've ever seen. He was serving khichdi at lightning speed, and when the pot was empty, a big truck backed up in front of him and a group of workers replaced the empty pot with a full pot of khichdi. The best analogy I can offer is that it was like watching a tire change during a pit stop at a NASCAR race. It was an incredible sight to see.

Yield: 4 servings
Prep time: 45 minutes
Cook time: 25 minutes in a pressure cooker or 70 minutes on the stove

---

EQUIPMENT
pressure cooker, optional

INGREDIENTS
1 mug of uncooked basmati rice

½ mug of dried black split gram lentils (see Tips)

ghee

1 large onion, thinly sliced

1 spoonful Ginger, Turmeric, and Garlic Paste (page 60)

sliced green Thai chili peppers to taste (see Tips)

½ cinnamon stick

pinch of black peppercorns

pinch of whole cloves

small spoonful cumin seeds

1 heaping spoonful of salt or to taste

1 spoonful unsalted butter, for garnish

small bowl of plain yogurt, for garnish

1. In a large mixing bowl, wash the rice and lentils using the washing technique for Basmati Rice (page 100). Allow them to sit in the water for 15 minutes.

2. Place a large pot over medium heat, add the ghee and onion and cook until the onion is golden brown, about 5 minutes. Add the Ginger, Turmeric, and Garlic Paste and cook until aromatic, about 2 minutes. Add Thai peppers, peppercorns, cloves, and cumin seeds and mix well.

3. Strain the rice and lentils and add them to the pot on the stove. Add salt and cover the mixture with water until it's about one knuckle above the surface. You don't have to be too precise as long as the grains are submersed.

4. Cover the pot with a tight-fitting lid and bring to a simmer over low-medium heat. Cook until everything is soft, about 45 to 60 minutes, stirring every 15 minutes. If you are using a pressure cooker, this takes about 15 minutes.

5. Serve immediately with a drizzle of melted butter and yogurt for garnish.

Lamb Pulao

There's a constant debate in my home: biryani versus pulao. Both are great rice dishes, but in my humble opinion, pulao is the clear winner. I love the simplicity of cooking rice in a flavorful stock—in this case, lamb stock. What looks like a plain rice-and-meat dish is the furthest thing from "plain." Its simplicity lies in the complex seasonings. An array of spices shining through in every bite combined with refreshing raita creates the perfect rice dish: pulao.

Yield: 4–6 servings
Prep time: 5 minutes
Cook time: 85 minutes

INGREDIENTS

2 spoonfuls ghee, divided

3 pounds (1350g) (about 6 handfuls) bone-in lamb shoulder, cut into cubes using a cleaver

1 spoonful salt, divided

½ spoonful black peppercorns

1 spoonful cumin seeds

1 spoonful coriander seeds

1 cinnamon stick

½ spoonful green cardamom pods

½ spoonful black cardamom pods

½ whole spoonful cloves

2 onions, finely sliced, divided

2 spoonfuls Ginger, Turmeric, and Garlic Paste (page 60), divided

1 mug uncooked basmati rice, rinsed

Raita, for garnish (page 129)

1. Place a large pot over medium-high heat and add 1 spoonful ghee. Season the lamb with 1 spoonful of salt and add it to the pot. Sear the lamb on all sides until golden brown, about 2 minutes per side, remove the lamb and set aside.

2. Reduce heat to low and add the peppercorns, cumin seeds, coriander seeds, cinnamon stick, green and black cardamom pods, and cloves and lightly toast all until aromatic, about 2 minutes (see Tip).

3. To the pot, add half of the sliced onions, 1 spoonful of Ginger, Turmeric, and Garlic Paste, the remaining salt, and the seared lamb. Fill the pot with enough water to submerge the meat, cover, and bring to a simmer over low-medium heat, for 60 minutes. Taste and adjust the seasonings. Strain the stock, separating the lamb, and set both aside.

4. Return the pot to the stove over medium heat. Add the remaining onions, ghee, and Ginger, Turmeric, and Garlic Paste. Cook until aromatic, about 2 minutes. Add the lamb to the pot and enough stock to submerge it. Bring to a boil, reduce the heat to low, and add the basmati rice. Mix well and cook uncovered until the stock reduces by a third. Cover the pot and steam for roughly 10 minutes.

5. Serve immediately with a garnish of Raita (page 129).

TIP

Be sure to scrape the bottom of the pan after searing the lamb to remove residue left behind. This is where a ton of flavor lies. A wooden spoon or heat proof spatula work best to deglaze the remains, especially when liquid is added to the pan.

Biryani

Biryani is one of the most popular rice dishes in Pakistan and perhaps the world. My mother would often make biryani when expecting a group of people; typically, family and friends coming over and making memories while gathering around great food. Biryani feeds the masses, even the pickiest eaters. I hope you enjoy this Biryani as much as I do!

Yield: 6 servings
Prep time: 40 minutes
Cook time: 45 minutes

INGREDIENTS

4 skinless bone-in chicken quarters, thighs and legs separated and chopped into large chunks with a cleaver

1 spoonful salt

4 spoonfuls, plain yogurt

1 spoonful chili powder

1 spoonful Garam Masala (see page 20)

2 spoonfuls Ginger, Turmeric, and Garlic Paste (see page 60)

handful of dried plums, kept whole

1 spoonful ghee

2 medium onions, thinly sliced

2 large potatoes, cubed

sliced green Thai chili peppers, to taste (see Tips)

1 medium tomato, sliced, divided

1 spoonful saffron, optional

half a palmful of fresh mint leaves

palmful of chopped cilantro

squeeze of fresh lemon juice

Raita, for garnish (see page 129)

1 mug uncooked basmati rice, washed according to instructions on page 100

1. In a large mixing bowl, combine the chicken, salt, and yogurt and mix well to evenly coat the chicken. Add the chili powder, garam masala, Ginger, Turmeric, and Garlic Paste, and dried plums. Mix well and then place in the fridge to marinate for a minimum of 30 minutes.

2. Place a large pot over medium-high heat, add the ghee and onions, and sauté until caramelized and golden brown, about 5 minutes. To the pot, add the chicken with the marinade, potatoes, Thai peppers, and half the tomatoes. Mix well, cover, and cook over medium heat for 10 minutes.

3. Prepare and cook the rice as according to the instructions on page 100 and then set it aside.

4. Combine the saffron, if using, with a few spoonfuls of water and allow the saffron to infuse the water.

5. To assemble the biryani, transfer half of the chicken to a plate and set aside. There should be a layer of chicken at the bottom of the pot. With a large spoon, gently add a layer of rice on top of the chicken in the pot, just enough so it covers the layer of chicken. Drizzle half of the saffron water over the rice and cover with remaining sliced tomatoes, mint, and cilantro. Then place the chicken from the plate over the top layer and repeat the process until you've used all of the ingredients.

6. Place the pot back on the stove over low heat. Cover the pot with a tight-fitting lid and cook for 10 minutes. Remove the pot from the heat and, keeping the pot covered, let the dish for 5 minutes.

7. Remove the lid, squeeze lemon juice over the top, and carefully mix the rice, pulling the chicken from the bottom to combine.

8. Plate biryani with rice, pieces of chicken, and potatoes. Garnish with Raita. Enjoy!

TIPS

✳ Green Thai chili peppers are spicy! Be cautious with how many you use. Try nibbling one to determine the heat and then add one or more according to your desired taste.

✳ Placing a clean kitchen towel under the lid creates a tight seal for steaming.

MAMA'S FAVORITES

"My mom used to make delicious food and I always watched her. I still remember how the dishes tasted. A lot of my family members like my cooking so I'm happy to be in a position to share the foods we loved growing up. I learned all my cooking from my mother and it's really hard to choose favorites. The ones I chose to share here were dishes that my mother made for me and that I took on to make for my children too." —Mama

Churi

Many mothers have lost feeling in their fingertips from the constant flipping of flatbread over very high heat. Churis are like Parathas (see page 38), except they are topped with brown sugar and ghee. They're still one of mine and my brother's favorite treats since we were about 5 years old. It's shocking that my mother still has feeling in her fingertips with all her time flipping churis—she has a higher pain tolerance than I do!

Yield: 2 churis
Prep time: 50 minutes
Cook time: 6 minutes

EQUIPMENT
tawa or any flat pan, like a
    crêpe pan
rolling pin

INGREDIENTS
1 saucer plate of atta (page 23),
    plus extra for prep
pinch of salt
glug of vegetable oil
a few heaping spoonfuls of
    butter, room temperature
ghee, for garnish
brown sugar, for garnish

1. In a medium mixing bowl, add the atta and salt and then mix it with your fingertips. Fill a pitcher of water and keep it on standby. Add about a cup of water and mix it with the flour using your hands. Continue adding water, a splash at a time, until a dry, well-formed ball is created. Cover the bowl with a dry kitchen towel and transfer to the fridge to rest for 15 minutes.

2. Remove dough from the refrigerator and transfer it to your clean countertop to begin kneading, periodically adding additional splashes of water if you feel the dough is too dry. Knead the dough until the end product is soft and smooth to the touch. Transfer the dough to a lightly greased plastic storage container or bowl, cover the container, and place it in the refrigerator to rest for an additional 20 minutes.

3. Remove the dough from the refrigerator and cut into two equal portions, about a palmful each. Lightly coat all sides of each portion with atta.

4. Hold the dough in your palm and, using the other hand, pull the perimeter of the dough into the center and repeat all the way around. Flip the dough to the opposite side. Cup the top of the dough with your other hand, and twist the dough to make a ball.

5. Press the dough into the plate of atta and form a disc. With your palm and fingers, gently squeeze the perimeter of the dough to flatten. Firmly hold the top and bottom of the disc and gently pull to elongate the dough while lightly slapping it against the countertop to shape it.

6. Using your fingertips, scoop out small amounts of butter, and evenly dollop the butter across the top side of the dough.

7. Hold both ends of the dough, and roll it from the top, with the buttered-side in, toward the bottom to form a log. Using both hands, carefully roll out the dough with your palms until each is the width of a pencil.

8. Take the length of dough and coil it into itself, like a snake, while periodically pressing the center to hold the coil together. This process is how the flaky texture of paratha is created.

9. Place the disc on your countertop or cutting board and, using a rolling pin, roll the dough into a circle. You should be able to easily hold it with your hands without the paratha tearing apart.

10. Preheat a tawa over medium-high heat until you see a bit of smoke. Carefully transfer the first paratha to the pan and generously add ghee to cover the top. Cook the paratha until the top has completely changed color, about 2 minutes. Flip the churi and cover the opposite surface with ghee.

11. Periodically rotate the churi to ensure even cooking. As the paratha cooks, fold it in half to create creases which creates extra-crispy churi.

12. Continue cooking the churi until all sides are golden brown and crispy.

13. Repeat steps 10–12 to cook the remaining churi.

14. Transfer the paratha to a plate, drizzle them with additional ghee, and sprinkle brown sugar over the ghee to taste. While it's still warm, rip and crumble the paratha while mixing it with the brown sugar until it's all chunky crumbs. Enjoy immediately.

Sweet Eggs

This is one of the first dishes I remember eating. I was born with a sweet tooth, and I was also a very picky eater. To satisfy my sweet tooth and incredibly picky eating habits, my mother would add sugar to my scrambled eggs—creating Sweet Eggs. This dish is quite nostalgic and memories flood back whenever I make it. If you have a picky eater in your home, you may want to give this recipe a try.

Yield: 2 servings
Prep time: 3 minutes
Cook time: 8 minutes

INGREDIENTS

4 eggs
pinch of granulated sugar
pinch of ground cardamom
knob of butter

1. To a small bowl, add the eggs, sugar, and ground cardamom and then whisk well to combine.

2. Warm a sauté pan over low-medium heat. Add the butter to the pan and melt to coat its surface before adding the egg mixture. Using a heatproof spatula or wooden spoon, stir mixture constantly until the eggs come together and are fully scrambled, about 2 to 3 minutes. Depending how you prefer your eggs you may cook this on the runnier side or more well done. Remove from heat and enjoy immediately.

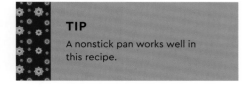

TIP
A nonstick pan works well in this recipe.

Anda Paratha

Anda (eggs) and paratha (crispy flatbread) is the quintessential breakfast dish for many Pakistanis. Pair this meal with chai and it's a perfect combination to start the day. I grew up eating this dish, and we are still making it today—and will continue until I am old and grey.

Yield: 2 servings
Prep time: 15 minutes
Cook time: 6 minutes

INGREDIENTS

4 eggs

pinch of salt

pinch of chili powder

small pinch of black caraway seeds/nigella seeds

1 green Thai chili pepper or to taste, diced (see Tips)

1 green onion or to taste, green and white parts thinly sliced

pinch of chopped fresh cilantro

knob of butter

2 Parathas (page 38)

1. In a small mixing bowl, add the eggs, salt, chili powder, caraway seeds, Thai chili pepper, green onion, and cilantro, and whisk well to combine.

2. Warm a pan over medium heat, add butter to the pan and allow it to melt and coat the pan, then pour the egg mixture into the pan. Cook the mixture, until the eggs create a crust and are golden brown on the bottom side (see Tips). Flip the egg patty and cook until the other side is golden brown, too.

3. Transfer the egg to a plate, and enjoy with Paratha, (and chai, if desired, see Drinks chapter page 190).

TIPS

* You can help the eggs set by pushing and dragging the eggs from the outside towards the middle of the pan at the beginning of the cooking process.

* Green Thai chili peppers are spicy! Be cautious with how many you use. Try nibbling one to determine the heat and then add one or more according to your desired taste.

Baingan ka Bharta

Not only is this one of my mother's favorite dishes, but it's also one of mine. If you've ever enjoyed the Middle Eastern dish baba ganoush, Baingan ka Bharta is very similar to it, but unlike a dip or appetizer-type dish, this is a main course. Also, this Pakistani version is spicier and, in my opinion, better.

Yield: 4 servings
Prep time: 5 minutes
Cook time: 50 minutes

INGREDIENTS

1 large eggplant

salt, to taste

freshly cracked black pepper, to taste

8 garlic cloves, peeled

glug of olive oil

glug of vegetable oil

1 medium onion, sliced

1 medium tomato, diced

1 green Thai chili pepper or to taste, diced (see Tips)

pinch of mustard seeds

pinch of fenugreek seeds

pinch of sesame seeds

pinch of unsweetened shredded coconut

pinch of black caraway seeds

½ spoonful cumin seeds

½ spoonful ground cumin

½ spoonful ground coriander

½ spoonful chili powder

small bowl of plain yogurt

1. Preheat oven to 400°F (204°C)

2. Slice the eggplant lengthwise and score the flesh in a criss-cross pattern deep enough to allow the seasonings to penetrate. Season the eggplant halves with salt and black pepper, and stuff the garlic cloves into the scores. Generously cover with olive oil.

3. Place eggplant, flesh-side up, onto a parchment paper–lined baking sheet, place it into the oven, and cook until fork-tender, about 40 minutes. Remove the baking sheet from the oven and set aside until the eggplant is cool to the touch. Once cooled, scoop the flesh into a bowl. Set aside.

4. Warm a medium saucepan over medium heat, and add the onion, tomato, and green Thai chili. Cook for a few minutes until the vegetables begin to soften, then add the mustard seeds, fenugreek seeds, sesame seeds, shredded coconut, caraway seeds, cumin seeds, ground cumin, ground coriander, chili powder, and additional salt, to taste. Allow everything to cook together for a few more minutes.

5. Add the cooked eggplant to the pan and mix well. Heat until the eggplant is warmed through and then remove the pan from heat and set aside. Add spoonfuls of yogurt, to taste, and mix well (see Tips).

6. Serve immediately with Roti (page 28) or rice.

TIPS

✻ Green Thai chili peppers are spicy! Be cautious with how many you use. Try nibbling one to determine the heat and then add one or more according to your desired taste.

✻ The more yogurt you add, the milder the final product will be. Remember to always taste your food as you go.

CONDIMENTS

A good sauce or garnish can make the meal. Without it, the dish may seem a bit incomplete. For example, when eating a delicious Lamb Pulao (see page 104), you need some acidity to offset the richness from the lamb, that's where a refreshing Raita (see page 129) can come in. These condiments should be a staple in your fridge and can also be used to spice up all kinds of dishes.

Mint Chutney

I'm not a huge fan of ketchup. I find its sweetness overwhelming, and it tastes artificial. Plus, there are better condiment options. I would happily choose Mint Chutney over ketchup every day of the week. Mint Chutney may be the most popular condiment used in Pakistani homes and is popular when served with kabobs, samosas, chaat, pakoras...and the list goes on.

Yield: 4–6 servings, as a condiment
Prep time: 5 to 10 minutes
Cook time: None

EQUIPMENT
food processor or mortar and
　　pestle (see Tips)

INGREDIENTS
1 small bunch fresh mint leaves,
　　tough stems discarded

1 small bunch fresh cilantro

salt, to taste

freshly cracked black pepper, to
　　taste

1 green Thai chili pepper, to taste
　　(see Tips)

squeeze of fresh lemon juice

plain yogurt, to taste

1. In a food processor, add the mint, cilantro, salt, pepper, Thai pepper, and lemon juice and then pulse ingredients until a thick green paste is formed. Transfer the paste to a mixing bowl and then add spoonfuls of plain yogurt, to taste, until yogurt and paste are well combined. Yogurt will calm the level of heat; remember to taste as you go.

2. Use chutney immediately or transfer to an airtight container and refrigerate for up to 3 days.

TIPS
* If using a mortar and pestle, start with the mint, cilantro, salt, and black pepper. Grind until a paste is formed. Add green Thai chili pepper and lemon juice and continue grinding until you achieve your desired consistency. Then, continue the recipe in the mixing bowl.

* Green Thai chili peppers are spicy! Be cautious with how many you use. Try nibbling one to determine the heat and then add one or more according to your desired taste.

Mango Chutney

Mango Chutney is my favorite chutney—it helps that mango is one of my favorite fruits. It has a great balance of sweetness, spiciness, and acidity, and it pairs perfectly with grilled beef or chicken kabobs. Mango Chutney uses green mango, which is generally available all year round.

Yield: 4–6 servings, as a condiment
Prep time: 5 to 10 minutes
Cook time: None

EQUIPMENT

food processor or mortar and pestle

INGREDIENTS

1 small bunch fresh mint leaves, tough stems discarded

pinch salt, to taste

2 pinches jaggery, to taste

1 green mango, peeled and diced

1 green Thai chili pepper or more to taste (see Tip)

squeeze of fresh lime juice

1. In a food processor, combine mint, salt, sugar, mango, Thai pepper, and lime juice, and pulse ingredients to the desired consistency. (If using mortar and pestle, begin by mashing the mint leaves, salt, and sugar. Then, add mango, Thai peppers, and lime juice and mash to achieve your desired consistency.)

2. Enjoy immediately or transfer chutney to an airtight container and refrigerate for up to 3 days.

TIP
Green Thai chili peppers are spicy! Be cautious with how many you use. Try nibbling one to determine the heat and then add one or more according to your desired taste.

Imlee Chutney

I think this chutney may be the only time I eat imlee, also known as tamarind. I don't use imlee often, but it makes one hell of a great chutney. Imlee Chutney is on the sweeter side and pairs well with most dishes, but it is crucial in Bun Kabobs (page 145).

Yield: 4–6 servings, as a condiment
Prep time: 5 to 10 minutes
Cook time: None

INGREDIENTS

2 large spoonfuls of tamarind paste
1 small spoonful of jaggery
pinch of chili powder
pinch of ground cumin
pinch of ground coriander
pinch of salt

1. In a small saucepan over high heat, add the tamarind paste and enough water to submerge the paste completely. Bring the mixture to a boil and then reduce the heat to medium-low and keep at a simmer. Continue cooking the until mixture is thick, but still able to fall off the back of a spoon.

2. Strain the mixture through a fine-mesh strainer into a small bowl and be sure to scrape the remaining tamarind from the bottom of the strainer.

3. Transfer the strained tamarind into a saucepan and warm over low heat. Add the jaggery, chili powder, ground cumin, ground coriander, and salt to the tamarind sauce and mix well to combine. Cook until mixture is aromatic and warm, about 5 minutes.

4. Serve immediately or transfer to an airtight container and refrigerate for up to 3 days.

TIP
This chutney freezes well. Store in an airtight container for up to 3 months.

Raita

Raita is a must-have for many rice dishes: it helps cut through the richness in Lamb Pulao; it's the perfect topping for Biryani; and it can add the "wow factor" to a relatively bland dish, like chana chawal (chickpea rice)—sorry, Mama. Some dishes are great on their own, but when they're topped off with Raita, it takes them to another level.

Yield: 2 cups
Prep time: 10 minutes
Cook time: None

INGREDIENTS

1 cup (8 oz) plain yogurt

1 pinch of ground cumin

1 pinch of ground coriander

1 pinch of salt

freshly cracked black pepper, to taste

squeeze of fresh lemon juice

¼ cucumber, finely diced

1 small tomato, finely diced

1 green onion, green and white parts finely chopped

½ small onion, finely diced

1 green Thai chili pepper or to taste, finely chopped, (see Tips)

1. In a bowl, combine yogurt, cumin, coriander, salt, pepper, and lemon juice and then mix well to combine.

2. Add cucumber, tomato, green onions, and onion to the yogurt mixture and stir until combined. Taste and adjust seasonings as desired.

3. Serve immediately or transfer to an airtight container and refrigerate for up to 3 days.

TIPS

* Toasting spices before using adds another flavor dimension to your food. Toast spices in a small sauté pan over low-medium heat. Stir spices constantly, toasting until aromatic, about 2 minutes. Remove the pan from heat and cool to room temperature. Use in your favorite dishes.

* Green Thai chili peppers are spicy! Be cautious with how many you use. Try nibbling one to determine the heat and then add one or more according to your desired taste.

STREET FOOD

Walk down any busy street in Pakistan and you'll find at least one of these dishes being sold in a stall. When you think about street food, you generally think of something quick, because you're on the go and you just need to eat and move about your day. But, when you're the one that has to cook it, and you're at home... it may not be as quick. You're going to experience a lot of different flavors in every little bite, so savor them because before you know it, they'll be gone.

Chaat Masala Corn

The earliest memory I have of eating corn was as a young child, enjoying it grilled with Chaat Masala sprinkled over top. A street food vendor on Gerrard Street in Toronto had a grill going on the sidewalk—he would grab a hot ear of corn and a lime wedge, which has been coated in Chaat Masala, and squeeze the lime all over the corn. I could eat this every day of the week.

Yield: 2 servings
Prep time: 5 minutes
Cook time: 10 minutes

INGREDIENTS

2 heaping spoonfuls Chaat Masala (page 20)

2 ears corn, husks removed

lime, cut into large wedges

2 knobs of unsalted butter, melted

1. In a mixing bowl combine all the spices and mix well to combine. Transfer mixture to a shallow dish and set aside.

2. Preheat the grill on medium-high heat.

3. Place the corn on the grill and, turning often, cook until it's golden brown on all sides, about 10 minutes.

4. Remove the corn from heat and brush with the melted butter to coat all sides.

5. Beginning with one wedge per ear of corn, dredge each side of the lime wedge in the chaat masala mix and slide the wedge up and down the cob, coating it evenly. Repeat with the second ear of corn. Enjoy!

MAKE IT YOUR OWN

Play with the ratios of the chaat masala ingredients to make it your own. A little more of one of the ingredients can transform the flavor profile to suit what you like best.

Pani Puri (aka Golgappa)

This dish has two names: Pani Puri (meaning water, fried dough) and Golgappa. It's one of the most popular snacks throughout Pakistan. When I'm in Pakistan I regularly see street vendors with carts full of prepared puris and bright spotlights shining down on them—at night the lights almost look like beautiful little lanterns. Filled with spicy and tangy toppings, Pani Puri is the ultimate one-biter. Think of it as a nacho with all the toppings, in one perfectly balanced chip. They are addicting, sorry not sorry.

Yield: 4 servings (makes 8 pani puri)
Prep time: 35 minutes
Cook time: 2 minutes

EQUIPMENT

rolling pin

small, round cookie cutter or small-rimmed glass

PURI

½ saucer semolina flour

1 heaping spoonful all-purpose flour

pinch of salt

½ spoonful baking soda

vegetable oil, for deep frying, plus extra for greasing the rolling pin

PANI

½ spoonful ground cumin

½ spoonful Chaat Masala (page 20)

½ spoonful mango powder

pinch of ajwain (carom seeds)

pinch of black salt

1 spoonful dried mint

pinch of salt

2 spoonfuls Imlee Chutney (page 126)

PURI

1. In a medium mixing bowl, combine the puri ingredients. Fill a small jug or pitcher with water. Continue mixing the dough, while periodically adding splashes of water as needed, just until the dough comes together. Knead the dough into a ball. The end product should be quite dense, and similar in texture to modeling clay.

2. Cover the bowl with a clean kitchen towel and set aside to rest at room temperature for 20 minutes.

3. Fill a large pot about ⅓ of the way up the sides with vegetable oil and set it over medium-high heat.

4. Using an oiled rolling pin, roll out the dough until it's thin enough to see through.

5. Using a small, round cookie cutter or a small-rimmed glass, cut out 8 circles from the dough.

6. One at a time, carefully transfer a dough circle to the heated oil and press down with tongs or a slotted spoon, which will allow the puri to puff into a ball. Flip the puri, and cook until golden brown on both sides, about 20 seconds total (see Tips).

FILLINGS

handful of chickpeas (canned or soaked and cooked, if dried)

handful of boondi (fried chickpea balls, they can be found at your local Pakistani or Indian market)

plain yogurt

7. Remove the puri from the oil and place on a paper towel to remove excess oil.

8. Repeat steps 6 and 7 to fry the remaining puris.

PANI

9. Add the pani ingredients into a medium bowl and mix with water. The consistency should be water-thin. Taste for seasoning and tanginess and adjust as necessary.

ASSEMBLY

10. With your finger, lightly poke a hole through the top of a puri, and carefully crack of bits of the puri to create a hole just large enough to fill it with toppings. You're essentially creating a little bowl, but it should be able to hold the watery puri mixture.

11. Add a few chickpeas, a pinch of boondi, a dollop of yogurt, and a couple spoonfuls of the pani mixture.

12. Immediately consume!

13. Fill the remaining puris as you're ready to consume them, or else they'll get soggy.

TIPS

* Many times we would simply buy the puri (fried hollow dough balls) at our local Pakistani supermarket. Feel free to skip the process of making it at home and save some time!

* The first puri should be a test run; adjust the time and temperature accordingly.

* To test if the cooking oil is ready, you may either carefully drop a small piece of flattened dough into it and see if the dough bubbles or dip a wooden spoon or chopstick and see if small bubbles form around it. If so, the oil is ready.

MAKE IT YOUR OWN

* Many people have slightly different variations of what they like to fill their pani puri with, but this is how we grew up eating it. Try adding pieces of boiled potatoes or some cilantro if you like.

MAKE IT YOUR OWN

Garnishes are all about preference. Typically, my family would have all the ingredients spread out onto the dinner table for us to choose our own adventure. Make it your own!

Dahi Baray

Dahi (yogurt) Baray (lentil fritters) is very complex. This dish is sweet, spicy, and tangy, with the most interesting spongy texture created by soaking the fritters in water. It may sound counterintuitive to soak fried food, but it seems to work perfectly in this dish. Growing up, this snack was a fan favorite in my house.

Yield: 2–4 servings
Prep time: 10 minutes
Cook time: 5 minutes

INGREDIENTS

1 mug white lentils, soaked overnight and drained

½ spoonful baking soda

pinch of salt

pinch of cumin powder

pinch of chili powder

vegetable oil

4–5 spoonfuls plain yogurt

splash of milk

½ spoonful Chaat Masala (page 20)

2 spoonfuls granulated sugar

½ small onion, finely diced

Mint Chutney (page 122), for garnish

Imlee Chutney (page 126), for garnish

semolina crackers, for topping (can be found at your local Pakistani or Indian market)

Pinch of fresh cilantro, for garnish

1. In a blender combine the lentils, baking soda, salt, cumin, and chili powder. Fill a small jug with water and begin adding water a little at a time to the blender to form a thick, smooth consistency. The mixture should hold its shape on a spoon when flipped upside down. Set the mixture aside.

2. Fill a large pot about ⅓ of the way up the sides with vegetable oil and set it over medium-high heat.

3. Scoop a heaping spoonful of the lentil mixture onto a spoon, then carefully push the mixture into the hot oil. Repeat with the remaining batter.

4. Fry the fritters until they're golden brown, about 3 minutes. You may want to flip these once while frying to ensure even cooking. Remove the fritters from the oil and transfer to a paper towel-lined plate to absorb any excess oil.

5. Fill a large bowl with water and add the fritters in. Allow the fritters to soak and become spongy, about 5–10 minutes. Squeeze the fritters to remove excess water and then set them aside on a plate.

6. In a small bowl, combine the yogurt, milk, chaat masala, sugar, and onion to create a gorgeous sauce.

7. To serve, spoon the sauce onto a plate, top with the fritters and more sauce, then garnish with the chutneys, crushed semolina crackers, and cilantro.

Samosas

Samosas, the king of all street food! Everybody loves these crunchy, fried, triangle-shaped snacks stuffed with all kinds of fillings, from vegetables to meat and cheese. Recently, I traveled to New York City to visit my good friend Saud and help with his pop-up restaurant—while there we created apple pie Samosas! They were incredible! Make these your own and fill them with whatever sweet or savory foods you and your family love.

My favorite Samosa, by far, is beef, especially when accompanied by a chutney.

Yield: 2–4, as a snack
Prep time: 40 minutes
Cook time: 10 minutes

EQUIPMENT
rolling pin

DOUGH
2 saucer plates all-purpose flour, plus extra for dusting

½ spoonful salt

2 heaping spoonfuls room temperature unsalted butter

pinch of ajwain (carom seeds)

FILLING
Keema filling (page 54); and/or Aloo filling (page 42)

1. In a medium mixing bowl combine the flour, salt, butter, and ajwain. Fill a small jug with water and begin slowly adding water to the bowl until the dough comes together to form a ball. Cover with a kitchen towel and set aside to rest for 20 minutes.

2. Tear off a golf ball–sized piece of dough and, between your palms, roll it into a smooth ball.

3. Place the dough ball into a bowl of flour and press, forming a disc. Transfer the disc to a clean countertop or cutting board and, using a rolling pin, roll the dough into a circle, similar to roti dough, but in a slightly oval shape.

4. Cut the circle down the middle to create two half circles of dough.

5. Using your fingers or a pastry brush, lightly coat the perimeter with water, this will act as the glue.

6. Lay one half of the dough flat on the palm of your hand with the brushed side up.

7. Lay your other hand palm-side up and lay on top of the dough. Your hands should now form a "T."

8. Push the fingers of your bottom hand upwards so the dough folds onto your top hand. Grab the dough with the thumb of your top hand and pinch the top to make a triangle seam.

9. Continue to fold the dough onto itself and squeezing the seams together to make a cone. You should have some excess dough draping from the perimeter of the opening.

10. Hold the dough like an ice cream cone and add spoonfuls of your filling inside the cone just below the top.

11. Squish the excess dough from the perimeter into each other to close the cone.

12. While holding, take both corners and join them together while connecting the seam down the middle to make a triangle. Transfer to a floured board or baking sheet.

13. Repeat steps 3–13 to create the remaining samosas.

14. Fill a large pot about ⅓ of the way up the sides with vegetable oil and set it over medium-high heat.

15. Carefully place samosas into the hot oil and cook until crispy and golden brown, about 8–10 minutes. (See Tips)

16. Transfer the samosas to a paper-towel lined plate or baking tray to absorb excess oil.

17. Serve immediately with Mint Chutney (page 122) or Imlee Chutney (page 126).

TIP

✳ To test if the cooking oil is ready, you may either carefully drop a small piece of flattened dough into it and see if the dough bubbles or dip a wooden spoon or chopstick and see if small bubbles form around it. If so, the oil is ready.

MAKE IT YOUR OWN

✳ There are many different types of samosas, some are thin and crispy while others are thick and crunchy with a bit of chew. Samosas can also have different styles of folding, the method demonstrated in this recipe is a very traditional fold, play with the thickness of the dough and folding styles to find what works best for you.

STEP 8

STEP 9

TIP

* ❋ Green Thai chili peppers are spicy! Be cautious with how many you use. Try nibbling one to determine the heat and then add one or more according to your desired taste.

MAKE IT YOUR OWN

* ❋ Size does not matter! Typically bun kabob are served as a slider, but on a recent trip to Pakistan I saw a stall using regular-sized brioche buns. Feel free to use whatever bun is at your disposal.

Bun Kabobs

Everyone loves a good hamburger, and this is the Pakistani version. Bun Kabobs are small, similar to a slider, but these are also vegetarian which means they are loved by the masses. I was first introduced to bun kabobs by my uncle Nana Mamu, these are his specialty. My entire family would venture over to Nana Mamu's apartment where he would serve dozens of Bun Kabobs for the whole family. Ah, memories.

Yield: 4 servings
Prep time: 5 minutes
Cook time: 25 minutes

EQUIPMENT
food processor

INGREDIENTS
5 egg whites, room temperature

1 mug split chickpeas (soaked overnight and drained)

1 large red onion, finely diced

2 small potatoes, cubed

2 spoonfuls Ginger, Turmeric, and Garlic Paste (page 60)

1 spoonful chili powder

1 spoonful Garam Masala (page 20)

½ spoonful cumin seeds

1 heaping spoonful salt

4 grinds of cracked black pepper

1 green Thai chili pepper, or more, to taste (see Tip)

palmful of chopped fresh parsley

squeeze of lemon juice

ghee, for cooking

slider buns

Mint Chutney (page 122), for garnish

Imlee Chutney (page 126), for garnish

1 small tomato, thinly sliced, for garnish

1. In a bowl, whisk the egg whites to soft peaks and set aside.

2. In a medium pot combine the chickpeas, onions, potatoes, Ginger, Turmeric, and Garlic Paste, chili powder, Garam Masala, cumin seeds, salt, and pepper and add enough water to cover.

3. Boil over high heat, then turn the heat to medium-low, cover with a tight-fitting lid, and cook until the chickpeas and potatoes are tender, about 35–40 minutes. All of the liquid should be evaporated.

4. Transfer the mixture to a food processor and add the green Thai chili, parsley, and lemon juice, and mix well to combine. Set aside and allow to cool.

5. Take a palmful of the chickpea mixture and shape into a small patty. Create the rest of the patties.

6. Heat a large nonstick pan on medium heat and add the ghee.

7. Evenly coat the patties in the egg whites just before adding them to the pan. Cook the patties until golden brown, about 1–2 minutes, flip and repeat. Transfer to a plate and set aside.

8. To assemble, add the chutneys to both sides of the slider buns and build in this order; red onion, patty, tomato, and finish with the top buns.

TIP

* Green Thai chili peppers are spicy! Be cautious with how many you use. Try nibbling one to determine the heat and then add one or more according to your desired taste.

MAKE IT YOUR OWN

* Feel free to replace the chicken with spinach and onions as this is another popular pakora variation. Mama would usually make this during the month of Ramadan for when we break our fasts and is one of my favorites. Follow the same method above and ensure the batter becomes quite thick so the spinach and onions almost clump together. Carefully spoon or pinch in clumps of the spinach/onion batter into the fryer and cook until they are golden brown.

Chicken Pakoras

Chicken Pakoras are the Pakistani version of chicken fingers. The pakora batter is universal and can be used to coat many different ingredients, including various meats and vegetables. During the holy month of Ramadan, my mother would commonly make batches of spinach pakoras to be eaten when we broke our fast. It's one of the most popular appetizers and one of my favorites too.

Yield: 2–4 servings
Prep time: 35 minutes
Cook time: 2 minutes

CHICKEN

vegetable oil, for frying

2 boneless skinless chicken thighs or legs, chopped into bite-sized pieces

1 green Thai chili pepper, or more, chopped (see Tips)

palmful of chopped fresh cilantro

fresh mint, finely chopped

pinch of salt

pinch of chili powder

pinch of Garam Masala (page 20)

splash of white vinegar

BATTER

1 saucer chickpea flour (besan)

2 spoonfuls Ginger, Turmeric, and Garlic Paste (page 60)

½ spoonful baking soda

½ spoonful cumin seeds

1 egg

½ mug buttermilk

FOR SERVING

Chaat Masala (page 20)

Lemon wedges

Mint Chutney (page 122)

Imlee Chutney (page 126)

1. a bowl, combine the chicken, Thai chili pepper, cilantro, mint, salt, chili powder, Garam Masala, and vinegar and mix to combine. Cover the bowl with plastic wrap and transfer it to the refrigerator to marinate for at least 30 minutes and up to 2 hours.

2. Fill a large pot about ⅓ of the way up the sides with vegetable oil and place it over medium-high heat.

3. In a mixing bowl, add chickpea flour; Ginger, Turmeric, and Garlic Paste, baking soda, cumin, egg, and buttermilk and whisk well to combine. Add water while whisking until thick pancake-like batter consistency is achieved.

4. Remove the chicken mixture from the refrigerator and liberally coat pieces in batter. Transfer battered chicken to the oil and fry until golden brown and cooked through, roughly 5 minutes.

5. Remove chicken from the pan and sprinkle with Chaat Masala and a squeeze of lemon juice.

6. Enjoy immediately with Mint Chutney (page 122) or Imlee Chutney (page 126).

SWEETS

It's a common Pakistani practice to enjoy these sweets during celebrations or holidays, but that doesn't mean you can't enjoy them at other times. The word "mithai" means sweet in Urdu. There are many mithai shops that focus solely on bite-sized desserts. When buying some, I would urge you to ask for a box that allows you to mix and match. Outside of mithai, you'll find sweet dishes in this chapter that aren't bite-sized and require a bit more preparation. After filling yourself up with a classic dish, these sweets will help to cool off your palette.

Kheer

As a child, I was drawn to super sweet desserts, but as I've grown older, I have migrated towards desserts with less sugar—Kheer is one of them. I've learned to enjoy its subtle flavor of cardamom, the texture and flavor of the rice, and its light sweetness overall. Give this recipe a try, and I promise you, too, will fall in love with it.

Yield: 4–6 servings
Prep time: 30 minutes
Cook time: 40 minutes

INGREDIENTS

1 mug uncooked basmati rice

pinch of salt

whole milk (minimum 3% fat but the fatter the better)

1 spoonful cardamom pods

1 spoonful crushed or roughly chopped almonds, plus extra for garnish (see Tip)

1 spoonful crushed pistachios, plus extra for garnish (see Tip)

1 spoonful shredded sweetened coconut

3 spoonfuls of granulated sugar

pinch of saffron mixed with water, for garnish

1. In a medium pot, pour in rice and enough milk to cover two knuckles above the surface of the rice. You don't need to be too precise. Place the pot over medium heat and bring the mixture just to a gentle boil and then reduce the heat to low.

2. Add the cardamom pods, almonds, pistachios, shredded coconut, and sugar, and mix well to combine.

3. Cook the mixture, mashing the rice grains from time to time with the back of a spoon, until the consistency is thick and similar to porridge or oatmeal, about 35 to 40 minutes.

4. Once it gets to this desired consistency, you're done. Remove the pot from the stove.

5. To serve, spoon the kheer into a bowl and garnish with almonds, pistachios, and saffron-soaked water.

TIP

Toasting nuts and seeds brings out their flavors, and it couldn't be easier to do. Place a dry sauté pan over medium heat and add your desired nuts or seeds. Cook until they are golden brown and aromatic, about 5 to 10 minutes, depending on the size of the nuts or seeds.

TIP

Based on the sizes of your saucepan and pot, be sure to eyeball how much water you'll need so the rice is submerged in the sugar water. Rice typically doubles in volume once cooked.

Zarda

During any celebration, whether it be Eid or a wedding, Zarda—also known as meethi chawal—is usually found on the table. Some may find it odd to eat sweetened rice, since it's commonly made in a savory way, but trust me, it's delicious.

Yield: 3–4 servings
Prep time: 30 minutes
Cook time: 20 minutes

INGREDIENTS

granulated sugar

pinch of cardamom pods

pinch of whole cloves

pinch of saffron

spoonful of turmeric powder or yellow food coloring, optional

1 mug uncooked basmati rice, washed according to instructions on page 100

1 spoonful salt

ghee

spoonful shredded sweetened coconut

spoonful of pistachios, roughly chopped

spoonful of almonds, roughly chopped

spoonful of cashews, roughly chopped

spoonful of raisins

spoonful of orange zest

1. In a small saucepan over medium heat, add enough sugar to make a thick layer at the bottom of the pan. Pour in just enough water so it submerges the sugar. Add the cardamom pods, cloves, saffron, and turmeric powder, if using. Bring to a boil and stir to dissolve the sugar. Remove from the heat and set aside. (See Tip.)

2. Cook the basmati rice with salt until halfway done (see page 100 for cooking instructions). It should not be crunchy, but it should still have a bit of a bite. Drain rice through a colander.

3. Using the same pot the rice was cooked in, add enough ghee to cover the bottom of the pot. Return the drained rice to the pot. Add enough sugar water so it submerges the rice.

4. Add the shredded coconut, pistachios, almonds, cashews, raisins, and orange zest and mix gently.

5. Cover the pot and simmer the rice over medium heat for roughly 5 minutes or until all the liquid is evaporated.

6. Plate and enjoy!

Gajar ka Halwa

Halwa is similar to pudding, and like pudding, there are many flavors of halwa. This version is made with carrots. In elementary school, we had a potluck meal where each family brought a dish that was handed down in their family through the generations. My mother decided to make Gajar ka Halwa. I'll be honest, I didn't really love it at the time because I was a normal kid and vegetables were not my jam. I also knew the other kids wouldn't like it for the same reason, and I was right. None of the other kids went for it, but all the teachers loved it! Once I was older, I learned to appreciate it. Gajar ka Halwa is sweet, floral, and nutty. I know you'll love it!

Yield: 6 servings
Prep time: 10 minutes
Cook time: 40 minutes

EQUIPMENT
food processor

INGREDIENTS
3 large carrots, peeled and shredded

pinch of crushed cardamom pods

granulated sugar

ghee

whole milk (the fatter the better)

handful of milk solids

large spoonful sweetened shredded coconut

large spoonful of cashews, roughly chopped

large spoonful of almonds, roughly chopped

large spoonful of pistachios, roughly chopped

1. Place a large pan over medium heat, add the carrots, stirring continuously, cook until the carrots are soft and most of the water has been absorbed or evaporated (see Tip).

2. Add the cardamom pods and enough sugar to evenly cover the carrots, reduce the heat to low, and cook until the sugar has dissolved, about 3–5 minutes.

3. Add enough ghee to evenly coat the carrots and then pour whole milk over them until they are covered.

4. Stir continuously until the mixture is bubbling and thick, about 15–20 minutes.

5. Add the khoya (milk solids), shredded coconut, cashews, almonds, and pistachios and cook until mixture is thick, about 5 minutes. The halwa should stick to your spoon for a few seconds when it's turned sideways.

6. Serve warm in small bowls garnished with additional nuts, if desired.

TIP

When cooking the carrots be sure to cook until the water has evaporated and they are soft—but no longer! Due to their high sugar content, the carrots can easily overcook, resulting in bitter or burned carrots. Ensure the water is gone but don't let the carrots dry out and stick to the pan.

TIP

Another common way to eat Sooji ka Halwa is by pressing it into patties and storing them in the refrigerator—
An instant portable snack!

Sooji ka Halwa

A classic Pakistani breakfast trio includes paya, chana, and Sooji ka Halwa—all eaten with puri. Growing up, my parents would take us out to a local restaurant to have Sooji ka Halwa for a treat. This semolina pudding was always the perfect dessert to complete my breakfast. When visiting Rawalpindi, Pakistan, I tried their famous halwa and puri, and I was happy to discover that the one we make at home is quite similar, if not better.

Yield: 6 servings
Prep time: 5 minutes
Cook time: 30 minutes

INGREDIENTS

granulated sugar

pinch of crushed cardamom pods

ghee

1 saucer of semolina flour

pinch of salt

drizzle of olive oil

spoonful of pistachios,
    roughly chopped

spoonful of almonds,
    roughly chopped

spoonful of walnuts,
    roughly chopped

spoonful of raisins

1. Cover the bottom of a medium saucepan with a thick layer of sugar. Add about twice as much water as sugar and the cardamom pods. Over medium heat, bring the mixture to a simmer and reduce the liquid until a thick syrup is formed, about 10 minutes.

2. Place a large pan over medium heat, add enough ghee to evenly coat the bottom of the pan, and sprinkle in the semolina flour to make a roux. Mix and cook until the roux turns light brown, about 5 minutes.

3. Carefully pour the syrup into the flour mixture and add a few spoonfuls of water. Continue cooking and stirring until a thick mixture has formed and the water has evaporated, about 5 minutes.

4. Season the mixture with salt and a drizzle of olive oil, then add the pistachios, almonds, walnuts, and raisins to the pan and mix. The end consistency should be a bit crumbly and similar to wet sand.

5. Enjoy warm in small bowls with Puri (page 46).

Falooda

Who wouldn't love a dessert that's a mix of ice cream, Jell-O...and noodles? This is the wild creation known as Falooda. It's a combination of a dessert and a drink. If you're familiar with Filipino foods, then you can kind of think of Falooda as a distant cousin of halo-halo. When I was younger, I would always grab Falooda with my family at a local Pakistani restaurant on Gerrard Street in Toronto on hot summer days. You commonly eat it with a spoon and a straw because as you mix and eat, it'll begin to melt. The addition of the noodles reminds me of the tapioca pearls in boba tea. There's loads of different flavors and textures going on in a serving of Falooda.

Yield: 4 servings
Prep time: 15 minutes
Cook time: 15 minutes

INGREDIENTS

1 box (6 ounces) flavored Jell-O (any flavor you wish), prepared and chilled

½ glass of whole milk

pinch of almonds, roughly chopped

pinch of pistachios, roughly chopped

¼ can (about 3.5 ounces) evaporated milk

hefty pinch of vermicelli noodles

dash of rose syrup

spoonful of basil seeds, soaked in water until thickened

ice cream, any flavor you like

TIP

There are many different flavors of and toppings for falooda. When ordering it, you commonly ask for what you want (or don't want) in it, so feel free to mix and match your favorite flavors and ingredients!

1. Cut the prepared Jell-O into bite-size pieces and set aside.

2. In a small saucepan, add the milk, almonds, pistachios, and evaporated milk, and bring the mixture to a simmer over medium heat. Set aside to cool.

3. Fill a medium pot with water and bring to a boil. Add the vermicelli noodles and cook according to the package directions. Drain the noodles and set aside to cool.

4. To serve, select a tall glass and drizzle rose syrup into the bottom and sides of your first glass. Then begin layering from the bottom beginning with a spoonful of Jell-o, a pinch of basil seeds, a small handful of cooked vermicelli, a scoop of ice cream, and a spoonful of the milk-and-nut mixture. Repeat the layers until the glass is full. Assemble the remaining 3 glasses.

5. Enjoy immediately using a straw and a spoon.

Rasmalai

You might think kulfi is my favorite dessert, and it's definitely up there. But if I had to choose one, it's Rasmalai. Essentially a sweet cottage cheese, Rasmalai has a great spongy and squishy texture. It also doesn't have to be made overly sweet—which is great for our community since many of the aunties in my life are struggling with diabetes. It's a great skill to be able to make the desserts you love at home because you can adjust the sugar so everyone can enjoy them.

Yield: 4–6 rasmalai
Prep time: 10 minutes
Cook time: 90 minutes, plus 60 minutes resting time

EQUIPMENT
cheesecloth

INGREDIENTS
spoonful of granulated sugar, plus more for syrup

small handful of almonds, roughly chopped, plus extra for garnish

small handful of pistachios, roughly chopped, plus extra for garnish

2 pinches of cardamom pods, lightly crushed, divided

1 pinch of saffron, plus extra for garnish

1 gallon whole milk (the fatter the better)

squeeze of fresh lemon juice, plus more for syrup

1. In a medium saucepan, add a spoonful of sugar, almonds, pistachios, 1 pinch of cardamom pods, and saffron, and then add half the milk. Place the pan over medium heat and stirring constantly, reduce the mixture by one third, about 30 minutes. Check sweetness level, adjust flavors as desired, and then remove the pan from the heat. Transfer to a container and chill in the fridge until ready to use.

2. In another pan, add the remaining milk along with a squeeze of lemon juice and slowly mix it in, letting it curdle the milk and create curds. If you don't see any curds forming in the first few minutes, you may need to add a bit more lemon juice. The curdling process may take up to 30 minutes to complete.

3. Once the curds have formed, immediately pour the mixture through cheesecloth, straining the liquid from the solids. Gently rinse the solids in the cheesecloth with running water to get rid of the lemon flavor. Don't squeeze too hard. Discard the liquid.

4. Tie the cheesecloth with the curds onto your sink faucet (so it can drain over your sink) and let the curds drain and rest at room temperature for about 15 minutes.

5. Transfer the curds from the cheesecloth to a medium mixing bowl and knead the curds into a smooth ball. Break the curd ball into smaller golf ball–size pieces and press each ball to form a cheese disc (see Tip).

6. In a lidded medium saucepan, add enough sugar to cover the bottom. Add about twice as much water as sugar and then add the remaining cardamom pods and squeeze the lemon juice over the top. Set the pan over medium heat and bring the mixture to a simmer. Keep the sugar water at a gentle simmer and reduce the liquid until a thick syrup is formed, about 5 to 10 minutes. There should be enough syrup to fully submerge the cheese discs.

7. Carefully add the discs to simple syrup and cover the pan. Reduce the heat to low, and simmer for 15 minutes or until the discs have swelled. Remove the saucepan from heat and set aside to cool for 15 minutes.

8. In a small baking dish, pour the reserved mug of milk mixture from step 1 into the bottom and then carefully place your discs in the dish. The discs should be about two-thirds covered by the milk mixture. Garnish each disc with additional almonds, pistachios, and saffron. Place the baking dish in the fridge and allow the rasmalai to set for at least an hour or as long as overnight.

TIP

When forming the discs, be sure they're as smooth as possible and that no cracks form. Cracks can cause the cheese to separate when cooked in the syrup.

STEP 4

STEP 5

Barfi

Think of this as our version of fudge. Growing up, this was one of the first desserts I enjoyed. Whenever I walked into a mithai (sweet) shop, they would have Barfi stacked up on top of each other in all different colors and flavors behind the glass. It was always a beautiful sight to see!

Yield: 6 servings
Prep time: 5 minutes
Cook time: 25 minutes, plus three hours to cool and set

INGREDIENTS

ghee

pinch of ground cardamom

whole milk (the fatter the better)

½ mug of milk powder

2 heaping spoonfuls of granulated sugar

edible silver flakes, for garnish (optional)

1. In a large pan over medium heat, add enough ghee to evenly coat the bottom of the pan and a spoonful of cardamom powder. Pour in about 3 times as much milk as there is ghee. Mix until everything is evenly incorporated.

2. Add the powdered milk to the mixture. Stirring continuously with a heatproof spatula, cook the mixture until it thickens to the point where it turns into a thick paste, about 20 minutes (see Tip).

3. Add the sugar and continue to stir and reduce the mixture. It's ready when you must shake your spatula to remove the mixture from it, about 5 minutes.

4. Transfer mixture to a small baking tray and level it out. Sprinkle edible silver over the top, if using, and place it in the fridge to set for at least 3 hours. It should have the consistency of fudge.

5. Cut Barfi into serving-size squares and enjoy.

TIP

Feel free to add more milk powder if the mixture is too wet and is not thickening up.

Jalebi

Jalebi may be one of the most iconic Pakistani desserts—the spiral-shaped snack seen in movies or restaurants resembles a funnel cake. Growing up this was one of my favorite desserts, and I recently tasted the best Jalebi I've ever had when I visited the city of Rawalpindi in Pakistan. Patrons were lined up on the sidewalk watching the cook squeeze spirals of the batter into hot oil. It was crispy on the outside, soft on the inside, and soaked in a sweet syrup. Nothing beats eating a fresh Jalebi. Be careful, they're quite addicting.

Yield: 6–8
Prep time: 10 minutes
Cook time: 15 minutes

EQUIPMENT
squeeze bottle or piping bag

INGREDIENTS
2 saucers of all-purpose flour
½ spoonful baking powder
drizzle of olive oil
4 spoonfuls plain yogurt
granulated sugar
pinch of cardamom pods
squeeze of fresh lemon juice
vegetable oil, for frying

1. In a medium mixing bowl, combine the flour, baking powder, olive oil, and yogurt and whisk well to combine. Add water to a small jug or pitcher and slowly pour water into the mixture until a smooth, thick batter is formed. Set aside.

2. In a small saucepan, add enough sugar to cover the bottom. Add about twice as much water as sugar and then add the cardamom pods and squeeze the lemon juice over the top. Set the pan over medium heat and bring the mixture to a simmer. Keep the sugar water at a gentle simmer and reduce the liquid until a thick syrup is formed, about 5 to 10 minutes.

3. Fill and large pot or sauté pan ¼ of the way with vegetable oil and set it over medium-high heat.

4. Pour the jalebi batter into a squeeze bottle or piping bag and squeeze the batter into the hot oil in a spiral shape. Cook the jalebi until it's golden brown and crispy, about 2 to 3 minutes (see Tips). Repeat this step until you use up all the batter.

5. Using a slotted spoon, remove the jalebi from the oil and transfer it to a paper towel-lined plate to absorb excess oil. Then move the jalebi to the saucepan of simple syrup and let it soak for a couple of minutes.

6. Serve immediately.

TIPS

* To test if the cooking oil is ready, you may either carefully drop a small bit of batter into it and see if it bubbles or dip a wooden spoon or chopstick and see if small bubbles form around it. If either occurs, the oil is ready.

* Orange food coloring is traditionally used in this batter but is totally optional. If using food coloring, add it to the batter at the end of step 1 and mix well.

* Leftover jalebi isn't the best; please enjoy while still warm from the oil.

TIPS

✳ To test if the cooking oil is ready, you may either carefully drop a small piece of dough into it and see if the dough bubbles or dip a wooden spoon or chopstick and see if small bubbles form around it. If so, the oil is ready.

✳ If saving leftovers, store Gulab Jamun in an airtight container with some of the syrup.

Gulab Jamun

Gulab Jamun are incredibly sweet, so one may be enough for you, or perhaps two if you're like me. Gulab Jamun are similar to donut holes or Timbits (for my fellow Canadians), but soaked in a very sweet, sticky syrup. One of the reasons I always looked forward to special occasions like birthdays or weddings—or just a Sunday visit to a friend's or family's home—is because we would typically bring Gulab Jamun.

Yield: 10–12 gulab jamuns
Prep time: 15 minutes
Cook time: 15 minutes

INGREDIENTS

1 mug powdered milk

2 heaping spoonfuls room temperature unsalted butter

½ mug all-purpose flour

½ spoonful baking soda

whole milk (minimum 2% fat, but the fatter the better)

dash of rosewater

vegetable oil, enough for deep frying

granulated sugar

pinch of cardamom pods

squeeze of fresh lemon juice

dash of rose syrup

crushed pistachios, for garnish

1. In a medium mixing bowl add the powdered milk, butter, flour, and baking soda. Slowly add whole milk and rosewater while mixing with your hands, just until a firm dough is formed.

2. Divide the dough into golf ball–size pieces and roll into dough balls. Transfer to a plate or tray, cover with a clean kitchen towel, and set aside.

3. In a large saucepan, add enough sugar to cover the surface of the pan and about twice as much water. Add the cardamom pods, a squeeze of lemon juice, and rose syrup, and bring the mixture to a simmer to dissolve the sugar. Continue to gently simmer until the mixture is reduced and a thick syrup is formed, about 3 minutes. Remove the pot from the heat and set the syrup aside.

4. Fill a large sauté pan about ⅓ up the sides with vegetable oil and set it over medium-high heat.

5. Carefully drop dough balls into the hot oil and cook until golden brown, about 5 minutes (see Tips). Remove the gulab jamuns from oil and transfer to the pan of simple syrup. Swirl them around and allow it to soak in the syrup for a couple of minutes.

6. Serve hot and garnished with pistachios.

Boondi ke Ladoos

Ladoos are classic sweets that are widely known and adored in Pakistan. They are mini fried dough balls with sweet syrup and ghee. There are many types of ladoos, and this one is called Boondi ke Ladoo. It's one that I commonly ate while growing up.

Yield: 6 servings
Prep time: 15 minutes
Cook time: 30 minutes, plus 30 minutes setting time

INGREDIENTS

store-bought boondi

granulated sugar

pinch of cardamom pods

squeeze of fresh lemon juice

handful of crushed pistachios and cashews, mixed

ghee, for coating

1. In a medium saucepan, add a thick layer of sugar, enough to coat the bottom of the pan. Add about twice as much water as sugar, as well as the cardamom pods and a squeeze of lemon juice. Set the pan over medium heat and bring to a simmer, cooking the mixture until it is slightly sticky, about 15 minutes. Remove cardamom pods from the syrup.

2. Add the boondi into the syrup, cover the saucepan, and cook over medium heat for 5 to 10 minutes.

3. Remove from heat and add the pistachios and cashews to the pan, as well as enough ghee to evenly coat the boondi. Allow the mixture to cool slightly. When the mixture is warm, grab large spoonfuls of the boondi and shape them into golf ball–size ladoos (see Tip).

4. Place the ladoos on a tray and transfer the tray to the fridge to set the ladoo balls for 30 minutes. Enjoy!

TIP

If you find the boondi aren't sticking together, there might not be enough ghee or sugar or the mixture is too cool. Combat this by returning to step 5 and putting the saucepan back over medium heat and adding additional ghee and sugar. Mix until everything is evenly coated, then try making the balls again while still warm. Don't forget that the balls will form a stronger bond once the sugar and ghee become cooler while setting in the fridge.

KULFI

Kulfi is basically like ice cream, and it's a very popular frozen dessert in Pakistan. It's primarily made with whole milk (and just a touch of cream), does not contain eggs, and is not churned. The addition of sweetened condensed milk adds a distinct flavor and texture because of the milk solids. Traditionally, you'll find kulfi made in long cone-shaped molds, but you can make them in any mold you wish or even pour it into a container to freeze and eat with a spoon. I've included some the traditional flavors, along with other must-tries that I've experimented with. I've made it a habit to create a new flavor every Saturday (my cheat day), so these are some of my top creations.

Malai Kulfi

This is the OG kulfi flavor. The key tastes are the sweetness and creaminess that milk adds. In my opinion, this is kulfi at its most essential. There are no other flavors to mask the unique milky taste. I was lucky enough to visit a friend of mine in Lahore and see the original method of making kulfi. It was quite the sight to see as they made their own sweetened condensed milk and khoya (milk solids) from scratch—all with only one ingredient: milk.

Yield: 4 kulfis (depending on the size of your molds)
Prep time: 5 minutes
Cook time: 30 minutes
Freeze time: 8 hours

EQUIPMENT

rubber spatula

freezer proof mold(s)
    or container

INGREDIENTS

1½ mugs whole milk of your
    choice (the fatter the better,
    preferably 8% buffalo milk)

splash of heavy cream

2 heaping spoonfuls
    powdered milk or thumb-
    sized knob of khoya (milk
    solids)

sweetened condensed milk,
    to taste

1. In a large saucepan. add milk, heavy cream, powdered milk or khoya, and a drizzle of sweetened condensed milk, and bring the mixture to a simmer over medium heat.

2. Continue to stir and mix until the mixture reduces and combines a bit, about 5 minutes. Continue cooking and stirring until the consistency is thick and smooth, about 20 minutes.

3. Taste for sweetness and adjust ingredients if needed. Mix thoroughly.

4. Pour the mixture into your mold(s) and freeze for 6 to 8 hours. Enjoy!

TIPS

* Some bottled whole milk will have fat built up near the top, this is kulfi gold! Be sure to add this to your mixture for an extra creamy taste and texture.

* Be careful not to add too much sweetened condensed milk as this can hinder its ability to properly freeze, resulting in a gummy consistency. Drizzle a bit at a time and taste as you go.

Mango Kulfi

This is the first kulfi flavor I ever had. I was in elementary school and leaving a local Pakistan restaurant with a long cylindrical mango kulfi in my hand. It's a classic dessert for me and will always have a place in my heart.

Yield: 4 kulfis (depending on the size of your molds)
Prep time: 10 minutes
Freeze time: 8 hours

EQUIPMENT
blender
freezer proof mold(s)
    or container

INGREDIENTS
1½ mugs whole milk of your
    choice (the fatter the better,
    preferably 8% buffalo milk)

splash of heavy cream

2 heaping spoonfuls milk powder

sweetened condensed milk, to
    taste (see Tips)

1 large sweet mango (if in
    season), seeded and flesh
    reserved, or 1 mug of canned
    mango purée

1. Add the milk, heavy cream, milk powder, a drizzle of condensed milk, and the mango flesh or purée to a blender and blend until smooth (see Tips). Taste for sweetness, mango flavor, and adjust accordingly. Blend again if adding ingredients.

2. Pour the mixture into your molds and freeze for 6 to 8 hours. Enjoy!

TIPS

* If you don't have sweet mangos then you can buy a can of mango purée, which is a great substitute. My favorite type of mango is the Pakistani Chaunsa mango, it has the perfect level of sweetness. Unfortunately it's only in season from June to August in Pakistan so outside of these months I find myself using the purée.

* Be careful not to add too much sweetened condensed milk as this can hinder its ability to properly freeze—resulting in a gummy consistency. Drizzle a bit at a time and taste as you go.

* The consistency should be smooth and thick but pourable, so start with small spoonfuls of powdered milk and add more to thicken the mixture if needed.

Spicy Mango Kulfi

My first memory of eating kulfi was at a local Pakistani restaurant. I couldn't have been more than 8 years old at the time. There was a deep cooler filled with kulfi in a variety of beautiful colors. All I had to do was slide the glass to the side and pick a flavor. It was magical, and the mango flavor I chose didn't let me down. After one taste, I fell in love. There's just something about the texture, chewiness, and sweetness that kulfi offers. Ever since that day, I've been hooked.

This recipe was inspired by the South American drink mangonada, which includes a type of spice blend called Tajin and a tangy, spicy sauce called Chamoy. When making kulfi, the main ingredient is whole milk, so ensure that by volume this remains the main ingredient.

Yield: 4 kulfis (depending on the size of your molds)
Prep time: 5 minutes
Cook time: 30 minutes
Freeze time: 8 hours

EQUIPMENT
    blender
freezer proof mold(s)
    or container

INGREDIENTS

1½ mugs of whole milk of choice (the fatter the better, preferably 8% buffalo milk)

splash of heavy cream

2 heaping spoonfuls milk powder or thumb-sized knob of khoya (milk solids)

sweetened condensed milk, to taste

1 large sweet mango (if in season), seeded and flesh reserved, or 1 mug of canned mango purée

1 spoonful Tajin seasoning

drizzle of Chamoy

¾ habanero pepper, chopped (see Tips)

1. Place a large saucepan over medium heat and add the milk, heavy cream, powdered milk or khoya, and the sweetened condensed milk. Bring the mixture to a simmer and continue cooking, stirring, for 2 minutes (see Tips).

2. Add a pinch of Tajin and the habanero pepper. Mix well and continue cooking for for 20–30 minutes until the consistency is thick and smooth. Stir often and taste for sweetness. Remove the pan from the heat and let the mixture come to room temperature.

3. Add the mango pulpa and a drizzle of Chamoy and mix well. Taste and adjust as desired, we want the main flavor profile to be mango with a kick of heat.

4. Add the mixture to a blender and blend until thick and smooth.

5. Pour the mixture into your selected molds and freeze for 6 to 8 hours. Enjoy!

TIPS

* Habanero peppers are spicy! Be cautious with them. Try nibbling one to determine the heat and then add according to your desired taste.

* Be sure to scrape the pan while stirring constantly with a heatproof rubber spatula or you risk burning the mixture.

* If your kulfi ends up too chunky after cooking it, you reduced it too much, leaving only milk solids. There's a fine line between it being thick and smooth and turning into chunky solids. Be sure to stop the cooking process once it's thick and smooth!

* When blending hot liquids, remove the middle plastic cap of the blender top to allow the steam to escape. If need be, wait until the mixture has come to room temperature before blending.

Strawberry Kulfi

Growing up, I could only remember there being a handful of kulfi flavors. Strawberry was one of them. This flavor was highly suggested throughout my social media comments—who doesn't love strawberries?

Yield: 4 kulfis (depending on the size of your molds)
Prep time: 10 minutes
Cook time: 8 hours

EQUIPMENT
blender

freezer proof mold(s)
    or container

INGREDIENTS
1½ mugs whole milk of your
    choice (the fatter the better,
    preferably 8% buffalo milk)

splash of heavy cream

2 heaping spoonfuls milk powder

sweetened condensed milk,
    to taste

fresh strawberries, rinsed, tops
    removed and finely chopped

1. Add the milk, heavy cream, powdered, a drizzle of condensed milk, and strawberries to a blender and blend until smooth. Taste the mixture for sweetness and strawberry flavor and adjust the condensed milk and strawberries accordingly. Blend again if adding ingredients (see Tips).

2. Pour the mixture into your molds and freeze for 6 to 8 hours. Enjoy!

TIPS
* Feel free to mix up the sweetness and flavor profile by adding a bit of hot honey (in addition to the condensed milk).

* Be careful not to add too much sweetened condensed milk as this can hinder its ability to properly freeze, resulting in a gummy consistency. Drizzle a bit at a time and taste as you go.

* If you're a fan of cheesecake, add a couple spoonfuls of room-temperature cream cheese, a few pinches of granulated sugar, and a sprinkle of graham cracker crumbs to the blender before mixing.

Pistachio Kulfi

Good ol' pistachio—this was the first kulfi recipe I uploaded online. Pistachio Kulfi is where it all started! It was January 9, 2021, which was a Saturday (it's my cheat day). At the time, I never thought I'd make a whole series of kulfi recipes, but look at us now! After Mango Kulfi, Pistachio is my favorite classic flavor, and it's my mother's favorite, too, which is why I had to include it here. The nuttiness of pistachio works so well with milk that it's hard not to like this combination.

Yield: 4 kulfis (depending on the size of your molds)
Prep time: 5 minutes
Cook time: 30 minutes
Freeze time: 8 hours

EQUIPMENT

rubber spatula

freezer proof mold(s) or
 container

INGREDIENTS

1½ mugs whole milk of your
 choice (the fatter the better,
 preferably 8% buffalo milk)

splash of heavy cream

2 heaping spoonfuls powdered
 milk or thumb-sized knob of
 khoya (milk solids)

sweetened condensed milk,
 to taste

large handful of crushed, shelled
 pistachios

1. In a large saucepan, add the milk, heavy cream, powdered milk or khoya, and a drizzle of sweetened condensed milk and bring the mixture to a simmer over medium heat. Stirring constantly, simmer for 5 minutes.

2. Add the pistachios and mix well. Reduce the heat to low and continue simmering and stirring until the consistency is thick and smooth, about 20 minutes.

3. Taste for sweetness and pistachio flavor and adjust ingredients accordingly.

4. Pour the mixture into your molds and freeze for 6 to 8 hours. Enjoy!

TIPS

* Feel free to add different types of nuts to the pistachios in the recipe. I love the combination of crushed almonds and pistachios!

* Be careful not to add too much sweetened condensed milk as this can hinder its ability to properly freeze, resulting in a gummy consistency. Drizzle a bit at a time and taste as you go.granulated sugar, and a sprinkle of graham cracker crumbs to the blender before mixing.

Cookies & Cream Kulfi

I've never met a person who doesn't like Oreo cookies. This may be the best "ice cream" sandwich I've ever had, and the best part is that unlike most kulfi recipes, the milk doesn't have to be reduced. Blending and freezing the ingredients is just as good a way, if not a better way, to create this kulfi. When I posted this recipe on social media, it won the hearts of millions across the globe. Oreo itself commented, "Safe to say, Oreo-approved kulfi :)."

For kulfi, the main ingredient is whole milk, generally, so ensure that by volume it remains the largest quantity ingredient. The key flavor and sweetness comes from the sweetened condensed milk, while the denseness comes from powdered milk.

Yield: 3–4 kulfis (depending on the size of your molds)
Prep time: 10 minutes
Freeze time: 8 hours

EQUIPMENT
food processor
freezer proof mold(s)
   or container

INGREDIENTS
handful of crushed Oreo cookies

1½ mugs of whole milk (the fatter the better, preferably 8% buffalo milk)

splash of heavy cream

2 heaping spoonfuls milk powder

sweetened condensed milk, to taste (see Tip)

pinch of salt

1. Add the cookies to a food processor and pulse until crumbs are formed and set aside.

2. To a blender, add the cookie crumbs, milk, heavy cream, powdered milk, a drizzle of condensed milk, and salt. blend until thick and smooth, not watery.

3. Taste for sweetness (see Tip) and Oreo flavoring and adjust both accordingly. Blend again if adding additional ingredients.

4. Pour the mixture into the molds (such as silicone muffin-top molds) and freeze for 6 to 8 hours.

5. Enjoy the kulfi on its own or make a kulfi sandwich by putting it between two cookie wafers.

TIP
Be careful not to add too much sweetened condensed milk as this can hinder its ability to properly freeze, resulting in a gummy consistency. Drizzle a bit at a time and taste as you go.granulated sugar, and a sprinkle of graham cracker crumbs to the blender before mixing.

TIPS

✳ If using a microwave to melt chocolate, pause the microwave every few seconds and mix the ingredients to avoid burning. Chocolate can go from solid to burnt quickly!

✳ Be careful not to add too much sweetened condensed milk as this can hinder its ability to properly freeze, resulting in a gummy consistency. Drizzle a bit at a time and taste as you go.

Chocolate Peanut Butter Kulfi

Some say this classic combination of flavors is unbeatable—I think it's definitely up there. Chocolate and peanut butter go hand-in-hand (unlike mint and chocolate). When I popped this out of my mold and took my first bite, I immediately knew this was going to be near the top of my favorites list.

The main ingredient is whole milk, so ensure that by volume this remains the main ingredient. The sweetness will come from the sweetened condensed milk, while the denseness will come from the powdered milk.

Yield: 4 kulfis (depending on the size of your molds)
Prep time: 10 minutes
Freeze time: 8 hours

EQUIPMENT
hand (immersion) blender

blender

freezer proof mold(s)
    or container

double boiler, optional

INGREDIENTS
handful of peanut butter cups,
    finely chopped

3 heaping spoonfuls of creamy
    peanut butter

pinch of powdered sugar

1½ mugs whole milk of choice
    (the fatter the better,
    preferably 8% buffalo milk)

splash of heavy cream

2 heaping spoonfuls milk powder

sweetened condensed milk,
    to taste

1 plain milk chocolate bar,
    for coating

1 heaping spoonful of coconut
    oil, for coating

1. Add the peanut butter cups, peanut butter, powdered sugar, and a splash of water into a medium mixing bowl. Whisk with a hand blender until a smooth consistency is formed. Adjust by adding additional water if the mixture is too thick or add extra peanut butter if it's too thin.

2. In a blender, add the milk, heavy cream, powdered milk, and sweetened condensed milk.

3. Add spoonfuls of the peanut butter mixture to the blender and mix. Taste for sweetness and peanut butter flavor and adjust accordingly for your preference.

4. Pour the mixture into any freezer proof mold, and let it freeze for 6 to 8 hours.

5. To make the chocolate shell, melt the chocolate bar and coconut oil together in a double boiler or microwave and mix until silky smooth (see Tips). Pour chocolate coating into a tall glass or container that will be able to fit a kulfi pop.

6. Dip the entirety of the kulfi into the melted chocolate and remove. Hold for roughly 30 seconds until the chocolate shell hardens. Enjoy.

Chai-Biscuit Kulfi

A classic drink combined with a classic cookie, what could be bad about that combination? The addition of Biscoff biscuit butter sets this flavor apart from any other kulfi. I'm often asked what is my favorite kulfi flavor. Although it's difficult to choose, Chai-Biscuit Kulfi definitely ranks first or second.

Yield: 4 kulfis (depending on the size of your molds)
Prep time: 5 minutes
Cook time: 30 minutes
Freeze time: 8 hours

EQUIPMENT
rubber spatula

freezer proof mold(s)
    or container

INGREDIENTS

1 batch of Doodh Pathi
    (page 198) made using whole
    milk (the fatter the better,
    preferably 8% buffalo milk)

thumb-sized knob of
    khoya (milk solids)

sweetened condensed milk,
    to taste

3 spoonfuls biscuit cookie butter
    (see Tip)

1. In a large saucepan over medium heat, add the Doodh Pathi, khoya, and a drizzle of sweetened condensed milk. The key sweetness comes from the sweetened condensed milk, while the denseness comes from the khoya. Continue to stir and mix until the mixture reaches a low simmer.

2. Add the cookie butter. Reduce the heat to medium, and continue to cook and stir until the liquid is reduced and the consistency is thick and smooth. Depending on how much milk you use and the size of your pan, this reduction process can take 20 to 30 minutes.

3. Taste for sweetness and flavor. Adjust your condensed milk, cookie butter, and Doodh Pathi according to your taste.

4. Pour the mixture into any mold you wish and let it freeze for 6 to 8 hours. Enjoy!

TIPS

✳ Biscoff biscuits are incredibly tasty and reminds me of my childhood. I'd suggest trying cookie butter. Even if you just lick it off your fingers, you'll love it!

✳ Be careful not to add too much sweetened condensed milk as this can hinder its ability to properly freeze, resulting in a gummy consistency. Drizzle a bit at a time and taste as you go.

DRINKS

I would've just had this chapter filled with different types of chai, but I couldn't leave out lassis, which are a refreshing yogurt drink. Coming back to chai, which means tea in Urdu. The word has a bit of mainstream use now thanks to coffee chains branding "chai-tea lattes." Don't ever say chai-tea, you're literally just saying tea-tea. But I highly believe once you make chai at home, those tea-tea lattes are just going to taste like milk and tons of sugar. Good chai requires quality tea and spices, along with numerous boils and simmers. You can't rush this.

Chai Mix

My mother has been making this one-pot chai mix for many years. Instead of pulling out your various spices every time you want to make chai, this already has all the flavor you'll need. The ratio of your mix should depend on personal preference. I prefer my chai mix as listed here, with cardamom being the largest amount, followed by cinnamon, and so on. Experiment and discover your ideal blend.

Yield: 4 large spoonfuls
Prep time: 5 minutes
Cook time: none

INGREDIENTS
whole cardamom pods

Ceylon cinnamon sticks

fennel seeds

whole cloves

ajwain (carom) seeds

1. In an airtight container (like a mason jar), begin by filling the container ¼ of the way with fennel seeds, the next ¼ with cardamom pods, the next ¼ with cinnamon sticks, and the remaining ¼ with a combination of cloves and ajwain seeds. Shake to mix well.

TIP

Some people also like to add their black tea to this mix. I don't prefer this method because I like to control exactly how much tea goes into my chai, depending on how many people I'm serving.

Regular Chai

This is my father's favorite go-to chai. It's on the milder side, so I often catch him drinking it both in the morning and at night—and for good reason, it's very refreshing. It does contain one of my favorite spices, cardamom, so I've always enjoyed this recipe with him.

Yield: 2 servings
Prep time: 5 minutes
Cook time: 15 minutes

EQUIPMENT
mortar and pestle

strainer

INGREDIENTS
small pinch of cardamom pods (see Tips), lightly crushed using a mortar and pestle

3 spoonfuls black tea or 3 black tea bags

milk of choice (I prefer whole milk but see the Tips below)

jaggery or granulated sugar, to taste

1. Fill a small pot halfway with water and bring it to a boil over medium heat.

2. Add the cardamom pods and black tea and allow it to continue to boil for a few minutes. Add milk until the mixture turns orange. Bring the mixture to a boil once again, then reduce the heat to low, and simmer for another 5 minutes. (See Tips.)

3. Add a few pinches of jaggery, mix it in, and taste for sweetness. Adjust sweetness as needed.

4. Strain your tea into your cups, discard the solids, and enjoy.

TIPS
* Lightly crushing the cardamom pods releases more flavor.
* For a stronger chai, allow the tea and spices to simmer longer, about 5 to 7 minutes.
* I find oat milk to be the closest whole milk substitute. Feel free to experiment with other milk alternatives. Chai should be for everyone!

Masala Chai

If you find yourself at any Desi's home and they offer you chai, get cozy, because they'll want you to stay and any attempts to leave will be futile.

Chai is for everyone, from all walks of life, and masala chai is one of the more popular versions out there. The great thing about this chai is that you can make it your own—mix and match the spice blend based on your preferences. Each time you make it, it'll be a bit different and that's the beauty. Swap out a spice or two, boil it for a bit longer—however you alter the chai, it's totally okay.

This chai is often served at get-togethers, before and after meals, and special occasions. There's really never a bad time to have chai. Given this is such a quintessential drink in Pakistani cuisine, if you can nail this, you're definitely in someone's good books.

Yield: 2 servings
Prep time: 5 minutes
Cook time: 15 minutes

EQUIPMENT
mortar and pestle

strainer

INGREDIENTS
2 (or more) spoonfuls of Chai Mix (see page 192), gently crushed using a mortar and pestle

3 spoonfuls of black tea or 3 black tea bags

thumb-size knob of fresh ginger, lightly mashed using a mortar and pestle

milk of choice (I prefer whole milk but see Tips)

jaggery or another granulated sugar, to taste

1. Fill a medium saucepan halfway with water, and bring it to a simmer over medium heat (see Tips.) Add a couple spoonfuls of the Chai Mix, black tea, and ginger and boil for 5 minutes to infuse the flavors into the water. Fill the pot with milk until it turns orange in color.

2. Bring the mixture back to a boil, reduce the heat to low, and simmer for another 5 minutes.

3. Add a few pinches of jaggery, mix, and taste for sweetness. Adjust sweetness as desired.

4. Strain the tea into your cups and discard the solids. Enjoy!

TIPS

✳ Once you get used to making chai, you'll learn your preferences for the perfect amount of water, milk, and spices to suit your palate. Practice makes perfect!

✳ Feel free to experiment with milk alternatives.

Doodh Pathi

This is my favorite chai. What sets this version apart is that there is no water used, only doodh (milk). The elimination of water makes this chai much creamier and more filling. I had the best doodh pathi of my life during my last road trip through Northern Pakistan. It was quite cold on our route to Hunza and we stopped for lunch. It's customary to serve chai after almost every meal, so we ordered doodh pathi—and oh, did it ever warm our bodies! This is my go-to winter chai.

Yield: 2 servings
Prep time: 5 minutes
Cook time: 15 minutes

INGREDIENTS

milk of choice (I prefer whole milk, the fatter the better for this recipe (see Tips)

2 (or more) spoonfuls of Chai Mix (see page 192)

3 spoonfuls of black tea or 3 black tea bags

jaggery (see page xx) or another raw or unrefined sugar (see Tips)

1. Fill a medium saucepan halfway with milk and bring it to a simmer over medium heat. Add a couple spoonfuls of the Chai Mix and the black tea. Reduce the heat to medium-low and continue to simmer for 5 minutes; the mixture will turn an orangey-golden color.

2. Add a few pinches of jaggery and mix well. Taste for sweetness. Strain the mixture into your cups, discard the solids, and enjoy.

TIPS

* Sugar really brings out the flavor in chai. Feel free to periodically add more sugar as it simmers and taste as you go to get the perfect amount of sweetness.

* Oat milk may be the closest whole milk substitute. Feel free to experiment with other milk alternatives. There's a chai for everybody!

TIPS

✳ Once you see the tea become a dark reddish color, you're pretty much done and should remove the tea from the heat. If you continue to cook and aerate it, it will turn brown. This isn't necessarily a bad thing; the taste will be the same, but you won't get that nice pink color at the end.

✳ Feel free to experiment with other milk alternatives, such as oat or almond milk.

Kashmiri Chai

Kashmiri chai is almost too pretty to drink. Almost. This beautiful pink-hued tea is garnished with slivered almonds and pistachios. It does take some time to make, so it's best if you plan ahead and make a large batch. There are quite a few versions of Kashmiri chai with flavors varying from sweet to salty. I had a wonderful salty version while visiting Skardu, Pakistan. The cooks added butter to their chai which I had never seen before. My preference is a sweet version, and that is what I've shared with you here. Enjoy!

Yield: 2 servings
Prep time: 5 minutes
Cook time: 40 minutes

EQUIPMENT
strainer

INGREDIENTS
6 spoonfuls Kashmiri tea leaves

pinch of cardamom pods, lightly crushed

½ Ceylon cinnamon stick

1 star anise

½ spoonful baking soda

½ spoonful salt

milk of choice (I prefer whole milk but see Tips)

granulated sugar, to taste

slivered almonds and pistachios, for garnish

1. Fill a medium saucepan halfway with water and bring to a boil over medium heat.

2. Add the Kashmiri tea leaves followed by the cardamom pods, cinnamon stick, and star anise. Turn the heat to low and simmer for 5 minutes. Add the baking soda and salt. (Baking soda causes a chemical reaction and eventually turns the liquid a dark reddish hue.) Simmer the liquid until it's reduced by half, about 20 minutes.

3. At this point the color should be dark red (see Tips). If the color is not red yet, add a bit more baking soda and tea leaves to the pan and cook a little longer. Add ice cold water to the mix, roughly 3 mugs' worth, and stir. Bring the mix back to a boil, then strain out the solids and discard them. Set the tea aside.

4. Place a second saucepan over medium heat and fill halfway with milk.

5. Once the milk has come to a simmer, add ladles of the Kashmiri tea liquid and stir to combine until you achieve a nice pink hue.

6. Add a few pinches of sugar and mix well. Taste for sweetness and adjust as needed. Pour the tea into your cups and garnish with slivered almonds and pistachios.

Kahwa

My first kahwa was from an elderly man in Peshawar, Pakistan, who has been making this beloved green tea concoction for over 30 years. He sits on a raised platform making kahwa to order, using water from a giant water dispenser, and crushing cardamom pods in the tiniest mortar and pestle I've ever seen. The flavor is one I'll never forget.

Yield: 2 servings
Prep time: 2 minutes
Cook time: 5 minutes

EQUIPMENT
strainer

INGREDIENTS
3 spoonfuls of Peshawari green tea leaves

pinch of cardamom pods, lightly crushed

pinch of granulated sugar or more to taste (see Tip)

1. Fill a medium saucepan with water until halfway full, and bring it to a boil over medium heat. Turn the heat to low and simmer. Add the tea leaves to the surface of the water, along with the cardamom pods.

2. Add a generous amount of sugar and continue simmering for 2 to 3 minutes. If you boil it for too long the taste will end up being bitter.

3. Strain the tea into your cups, discard the solids, and enjoy.

TIP

Another traditional way of enjoying Kawha tea is to omit the sugar. Instead, have a little bowl of gur (concentrated cane sugar) nearby and enjoy a little following a sip of tea. Take a sip and crunch on a piece of raw sugar.

Cake Rusk

Cake rusk isn't a drink at all, but the only time we enjoy these treats are with chai, so it only made sense to include it in the Drinks chapter. Think of cake rusk as Pakistani biscotti. You either take a sip of chai followed by a bite of cake rusk or dip the cake rusk into the chai and take a bite—but be sure not to leave it in the chai for too long or it'll break apart and be lost at the bottom of your mug.

Yield: 6 rusks
Prep time: 15 minutes
Cook time: 60 minutes

INGREDIENTS

3 eggs

splash of vanilla extract

½ cup granulated sugar

¼ cup unsalted butter, room temperature, plus extra for greasing

1 cup all-purpose flour

1½ teaspoons baking powder

TIPS

* Baking is a science and it's generally a good idea to be precise. Every time I've made this it has turned out great. If it doesn't work for you, I'm sorry, I can't be of any help because I am a horrible baker.

* Play with the types of flour used or ingredients tossed into the batter.

1. Preheat oven to 350°F (180 °C)

2. In a medium mixing bowl, whisk the eggs and vanilla. Add the sugar and butter and whisk all until creamy. Lastly, mix in the flour and baking powder until thoroughly combined.

3. With additional butter, grease the bottom of an 8-inch square baking dish or line it with parchment.

4. Pour the batter into the pan and spread it evenly with a spatula.

5. Bake the cake for roughly 30 minutes and remove the dish from the oven. Check the doneness with a toothpick—if it comes out clean, it's fully cooked. Set aside to cool.

6. Reduce the oven temperature to 325°F (162°C).

7. Once the cake has cooled to room temperature, carefully remove the cake from the dish and place on a cutting board. Slice the cake into rectangles to create rusks.

8. Place the rusks on a large baking tray. Place the tray in the oven and allow the rusks to bake for 10 to 15 minutes. Flip the rusks and bake for an additional 10 to 15 minutes, so each side gets a bit golden brown.

9. Enjoy with chai or store container for up to a month.

Lassi

Nothing beats lassi on a hot summer's day. This is a yogurt-based drink. It's creamy, frothy, and hits the spot.

Yield: 2 servings
Prep time: 5 minutes

INGREDIENTS

½ mug of dahi (curd yogurt) or plain yogurt

Water or milk

3 to 4 ice cubes

2 spoonfuls granulated sugar

malai or cream, for garnish

khoya (milk solids), for garnish

1. Add the dahi or yogurt into a blender along with a few splashes of water or milk, ice cubes and the sugar. Blend until smooth. The mixture should be quite thick, similar to a milkshake.

2. Taste the mixture for sweetness and adjust accordingly.

3. Pour the lassi into ice cold mugs and garnish with malai and crumbs of milk solids. Enjoy!

TIP

Other popular flavors include salty lassi, which is made by replacing the sugar with salt.

Mango Lassi

I remember drinking mango lassi as a child, and I've enjoyed it ever since, especially when the spring and summer months are upon us. Lassi is a yogurt-based drink and mango is probably my favorite fruit, so this is a perfect combination. You can also find this drink served in many Pakistani restaurants, and it hits the spot to cool your mouth from a spicy dish.

Yield: 2 servings
Prep time: 5 minutes

INGREDIENTS

½ mug of dahi (curd yogurt) or plain yogurt

a few splashes of water or milk

3 to 4 ice cubes

9 heaping spoonfuls of mango pulp

pinch of granulated sugar, optional

1. Add the dahi into a blender along with the splashes of water or milk, ice cubes, mango pulp, and a pinch of sugar. Blend until smooth. The mixture should be quite thick, similar to a milkshake. After blending, adjust the consistency by adding more yogurt, ice cubes, or liquid (water or milk) accordingly.

2. Taste the lassi for sweetness and mango flavor and adjust if necessary.

3. Pour into ice cold mugs and enjoy.

Rooh-Afza Limeade

This is another favorite summertime drink of mine. Rooh-afza limeade is on par with any refreshment I've ever had. It's made from concentrated rose syrup, which is super sweet and floral. I generally enjoy it with water or milk during Ramadan, just before breaking fast. In the summertime, I love Rooh-afza Limeade made with fresh lime and mint.

Yield: 2 servings
Prep time: 2 minutes
Cook time: 5 minutes

EQUIPMENT
cocktail muddler, optional

INGREDIENTS
granulated sugar, for rimming the glasses

1 lime, zested and then cut into wedges (see Tip)

splash of lime juice (see Tip)

2 spoonfuls of rooh-afza (can be found at your local Pakistani or Indian market)

4 fresh mint leaves

1. Add sugar and lime zest to a shallow saucer and mix them together. Rub the rims of your glasses with lime wedges to wet them and then dip the glasses into the sugar-zest mixture. Set the glasses aside.

2. Pour a generous amount of rooh-afza into each glass, so it completely covers the bottom of the glass, add lime juice and mint leaves, and gently muddle (or mash) the leaves to release the flavor.

3. Fill the glasses with water and mix. Taste for sweetness and adjust accordingly. Enjoy.

TIP

Feel free to try this recipe with lemon instead of lime. Another popular ingredient is to add some basil seeds at the bottom of the glass. After a few minutes, the basil seeds will thicken up the limeade and add a nice texture to the drink.